TEACHER'S PET PUBLICATIONS

LITPLAN TEACHER PACK
for
Ethan Frome
based on the book by
Edith Wharton

Written by
Jill Bloomf eld

© 2008 Teacher's Pet Publications
All Rights Reserved

Copyright Teacher's Pet Publications 2008

Only the student materials in this unit plan (such as worksheets, study questions, and tests) may be reproduced multiple times for use in the purchaser's classroom.

For any additional copyright questions, contact Teacher's Pet Publications.

www.tpet.com

TABLE OF CONTENTS - *Ethan Frome*

About The Author	4
Introduction	5
Unit Objectives	7
Reading Assignment Sheet	8
Unit Outline	9
Study Questions (Short Answer)	13
Quiz/Study Questions (Multiple Choice)	21
Pre-reading Vocabulary Worksheets	41
Lesson One (Introductory Lesson)	59
Writing Assignment #1	62
Writing Evaluation Form	63
Oral Reading Evaluation Form	67
Non-fiction Assignment Sheet	73
Writing Assignment #2	77
Writing Assignment #3	82
Group Project	84
Vocabulary Review Activities	86
Extra Writing Assignments/Discussion ?s	88
Unit Review Activities	91
Unit Tests	97
Unit Resource Materials	155
Vocabulary Resource Materials	175

ABOUT THE AUTHOR

Edith Wharton

There is an adage for writers which says, "Write what you know." This means that the best material for a writer is rooted in the writer's own experience. The depth and richness of Edith Wharton's writing is derived from her own life. Wharton was born in 1862 to a highly privileged family in New York City. Originally born Edith Jones, her surname is thought to be the one referred to in the idiom, "keeping up with the Joneses." Her family was socially well-connected and young Edith grew up among the social elite in New York, the epicenter of culture, arts, fashion, and style. Wharton developed a propensity for the arts--both written and visual--from an early age. An avid storyteller and illustrator, Wharton showed creativity as a child and young adult. Interior decorating was a favorite creative outlet for Wharton, as it gave her a means of artistic self-expression that was socially acceptable for a woman.

Wharton's highly privileged lifestyle afforded her with opportunities to travel abroad, which gave her a great deal of creative inspiration. Though she built an expansive estate in New England, Wharton maintained a residence in France. Wharton frequently entertained guests and invited friends who were among the greatest authors and artists of the day to her homes. Most notable of these friends was Henry James, an American novelist whose works explore themes similar to those in Wharton's writing.

While living in France during World War I, Wharton became involved in support efforts for the allied side. Wharton did not return to America to live after the war. During this period Wharton wrote some of her most celebrated works including *The Age of Innocence*. This novel and others such as *The House of Mirth* and *The Buccaneers* explores the issues faced by upper-class women at the turn of the 20th century. Marked by wit and irony, Wharton's works insightfully challenge the societal expectations for women. Wharton's novel *The Age of Innocence* was awarded a Pulitzer Prize in 1921; this is especially notable, as Wharton was the first woman to receive this distinction. Wharton died of a stroke in France in 1937, her lifetime spanning great change in American culture and society.

INTRODUCTION *Ethan Frome*

This LitPlan has been designed to develop students' reading, writing, thinking, and language skills through exercises and activities related to *Ethan Frome*. It includes twenty-one lessons, supported by extra resource materials.

The **introductory lesson** introduces students to the concept of a "framed" story observed by a detached observer. Students will observe a photograph of a stranger and create a biography for that person basing their invented biographies on visual evidence in the picture. Following the introductory activity, students are given the materials they will be using during the unit. Students also begin the pre-reading and reading work for the first assignment.

The **reading assignments** are approximately thirty pages each; some are a little shorter while others are a little longer. Students have approximately 15 minutes of pre-reading work to do prior to each reading assignment. This pre-reading work involves reviewing the study questions for the assignment and doing some vocabulary work for selected vocabulary words they will encounter in their reading.

The **study guide questions** are fact-based questions; students can find the answers to these questions right in the text. These questions come in two formats: short answer or multiple choice. The best use of these materials is probably to use the short answer version of the questions as study guides for students (since answers will be more complete), and to use the multiple choice version for occasional quizzes.

The **vocabulary work** is intended to enrich students' vocabularies as well as to aid in the students' understanding of the book. Prior to each reading assignment, students will complete a two-part worksheet for selected vocabulary words in the upcoming reading assignment. Part I focuses on students' use of general knowledge and contextual clues by giving the sentence in which the word appears in the text. Students are then to write down what they think the words mean based on the words' usage. Part II nails down the definitions of the words by giving students dictionary definitions of the words and having students match the words to the correct definitions based on the words' contextual usage. Students should then have an understanding of the words when they meet them in the text.

After each reading assignment, students will go back and formulate answers for the study guide questions. Discussion of these questions serves as a **review** of the most important events and ideas presented in the reading assignments.

After students complete reading the work, there is a **vocabulary review** lesson which pulls together all of the fragmented vocabulary lists for the reading assignments and gives students a review of all of the words they have studied.

Following the vocabulary review, a lesson is devoted to the **extra discussion questions/writing assignments**. These questions focus on interpretation, critical analysis, and personal response, employing a variety of thinking skills and adding to the students' understanding of the novel.

There is a **project** in this unit. Students select moments from the text and write alternative scenes to create a "choose-your-own-adventure" text. Students will revise Wharton's ironic choices.

There are three **writing assignments** in this unit, each with the purpose of informing, persuading, or expressing personal opinions or creativity. The first writing assignment asks students to select three literary terms, define them, and provide examples of them from *Ethan Frome* in a factual essay. The second writing assignment challenges students to write about three goals which they would like to achieve; they must define their goals and explain how they intend to achieve them. In Writing Assignment #3 students write a letter to students in the next class that will be reading *Ethan Frome*, persuading them that although the book was published in 1911, it is not a dusty, old, has-been book; it has value for readers today.

There is a non-fiction **reading assignment**. Students must read non-fiction articles, books, etc. to gather information about topics related to *Ethan Frome*.

The **review lesson** pulls together all of the aspects of the unit. The teacher is given four or five choices of activities or games to use which all serve the same basic function of reviewing all of the information presented in the unit.

The **unit test** comes in two formats: multiple choice or short answer. As a convenience, two different tests for each format have been included. There is also an advanced short answer unit test for advanced students.

There are additional **support materials** included with this unit. The **Unit Resource Materials** section includes suggestions for an in-class library, crossword and word search puzzles related to the novel, and extra worksheets. There is a list of **bulletin board ideas** which gives the teacher suggestions for bulletin boards to go along with this unit. In addition, there is a list of **extra class activities** the teacher could choose from to enhance the unit or as a substitution for an exercise the teacher might feel is inappropriate for his/her class. **Answer keys** are located directly after the **reproducible student materials** throughout the unit. The **Vocabulary Resource Materials** section includes similar worksheets and games to reinforce the vocabulary words.

The **level** of this unit can be varied depending upon the criteria on which the individual assignments are graded, the teacher's expectations of his/her students in class discussions, and the formats chosen for the study guides, quizzes and test. If teachers have other ideas/activities they wish to use, they can usually easily be inserted prior to the review lesson.

The student materials may be reproduced for use in the teacher's classroom without infringement of copyrights. No other portion of this unit may be reproduced without the written consent of Teacher's Pet Publications, Inc.

UNIT OBJECTIVES *Ethan Frome*

1. Through reading *Ethan Frome*, students will develop close reading skills and consider foreshadowing, irony, and "framed" narration in greater depth.

2. Students will demonstrate their understanding of the text on four levels: factual, interpretive, critical, and personal.

3. Students will learn how to set goals that are realistic and measurable. Similarly, students will consider how they define success and failure. As students consider these issues, they will also explore the balance between duty and personal ambition.

4. Students will be given the opportunity to practice reading aloud and silently to improve their skills in each area.

5. Students will answer questions to demonstrate their knowledge and understanding of the main events and characters in *Ethan Frome* as they relate to the author's theme development.

6. Students will enrich their vocabularies and improve their understanding of the novel through the vocabulary lessons prepared for use in conjunction with the novel.

7. Students will read aloud, report, and participate in large and small group discussions to improve their public speaking and personal interaction skills.

8. The writing assignments in this unit are designed for several purposes:

    a. To check and increase students reading comprehension

    b. To make students think about the ideas presented by the novel

    c. To encourage logical thinking

    d. To provide an opportunity to practice good grammar and improve students' use of the English language

    e. To encourage students' creativity

READING ASSIGNMENTS *Ethan Frome*

Date Assigned	Assignment	Completion Date
	Assignment 1 Prologue and Chapter 1	
	Assignment 2 Chapter 2	
	Assignment 3 Chapter 3	
	Assignment 4 Chapter 4	
	Assignment 5 Chapters 5 & 6	
	Assignment 6 Chapters 7 & 8	
	Assignment 7 Chapter 9 & Epilogue	

UNIT OUTLINE *Ethan Frome*

1 Introduction PVR Prologue & Ch. 1	2 Study ?s Prologue & Ch. 1 Writing Assignment #1 PVR Ch. 2	3 Study ?s Ch. 2 PVR Ch. 3	4 Study ?s Ch. 3 Oral Reading Evaluation PVR Ch. 4	5 Study ?s Ch. 4 PVR Ch. 5 & 6
6 Study ?s Ch. 5 & 6 Jigsaw Activity PVR Ch. 7 & 8	7 Study ?s Ch. 7 & 8 PVR 9 & Epilogue	8 Study ?s Ch. 9 & Epilogue	9 Non-fiction Reading Assignment	10 Understanding Symbol, Motif, and Theme
11 Goal Setting Writing Assignment #2	12 Writing Assignment #2, Continued	13 Non-fiction Oral Reports	14 Close Passage Analysis Writing Assignment #3	15 Writing Assignment #3, Continued
16 Group Project	17 Group Project	18 Vocabulary Review	19 Further Discussion	20 Unit Review
21 Test				

Key: P = Preview Study Questions   V = Vocabulary Work   R = Read

STUDY GUIDE QUESTIONS

STUDY GUIDE QUESTIONS *Ethan Frome*

Assignment 1
Prologue and Chapter 1
1. In what city is the story set?
2. Why does the narrator consider Ethan the most striking figure in Starkfield?
3. What does Zeena often receive in the mail?
4. What is Zeena's real name?
5. Why hasn't Ethan moved away from Starkfield?
6. Why is the narrator in Starkfield?
7. The narrator lodges with Mrs. Ned Hale. What is he hoping to learn from her?
8. What service does Ethan provide for the narrator?
9. For what reason does Ethan offer the narrator lodging?
10. What caused a premature end to Ethan's studies?
11. Why does Ethan sneak up and look in the church window?
12. What color is Mattie's scarf?
13. Why is Mattie living with Ethan and Zeena?
14. For what reason does Zeena say Mattie will discontinue her services?
15. What does Zeena say causes Ethan to be late?
16. How does Ethan feel toward Denis Eady?

Assignment 2
Chapter 2
1. What does Denis offer Mattie outside of the church?
2. What is "coasting"?
3. What happened to Ruth Varnum and Ned Hale while coasting?
4. When Ethan tells Mattie that people say it is natural for her to leave Ethan and Zeena, what is Mattie's response?
5. What does Ethan imagine is written on every tombstone in the family plot?
6. What does Ethan fantasize about Mattie while passing through the graveyard?
7. What is different when Ethan and Mattie arrive home from the church dance?
8. What surprises Ethan when Zeena opens the door to let him and Mattie in after the dance?
9. Why does Ethan say he has mill accounts to go over?

Assignment 3
Chapter 3
1. With specific memory preoccupies Ethan on the morning after the dance at the church?
2. In what business had Mattie's father been engaged?
3. How did Mattie obtain $50 after her parents left her impoverished?
4. What about Zeena's appearance startles Ethan when he returns from hauling wood?
5. Why does Zeena travel to Bettsbridge?
6. Ethan tells Zeena he can not take her to the train in Corbury Flats because he has to collect money from Mr. Hale for the lumber. Why does he regret this lie?

Assignment 4
Chapter 4
1. How does Zeena's absence affect the appearance of the kitchen?
2. On what did Ethan and Zeena agree when they were married?
3. What reason does Zeena give for becoming quiet like Ethan's mother?
4. Why does Hale ask for an extension to pay his bill?
5. What is different about Mattie's hair when Ethan arrives home from Hale's stable?
6. What does the cat knock off the table and break?

Assignment 5
Chapters 5 & 6
1. What is the only "drawback" to Ethan's contentment while sitting in the kitchen with Mattie?
2. How does Ethan react when he sees Mattie in Zeena's chair?
3. What had Ethan and Mattie previously planned to do the night the pickle dish was broken?
4. What topic of conversation does Ethan decide is vulgar after he brings it up?
5. About what does Mattie worry while sewing next to Ethan?
6. What does Mattie do when Ethan kisses the material she is sewing?
7. What does Ethan remember when Mattie goes up to bed?
8. Who is Jotham Powell?
9. What does Ethan want to say to Mattie with "his heart in his throat"?
10. What happens to one of the mares on the way to the wood lot?
11. Why does Ethan go to Michael Eady's place?
12. What surprise does Ethan receive when he returns home from Michael Eady's place?
13. What is Ethan's reaction to Jotham's refusal to stay for supper?

Assignment 6
Chapters 7 & 8
1. What does Ethan initially think when Zeena remarks that she is very ill?
2. What is Dr. Buck's suggestion for Zeena?
3. According to Zeena, what caused her to lose her health?
4. Ethan tells Zeena she is the wife of a poor man and they can not afford the girl she has hired. How does Zeena react?
5. What causes Ethan's sense of helplessness at the end of his and Zeena's conversation concerning Mattie?
6. What does Zeena discover while looking for her stomach powders?
7. What reason does Mattie give for using the pickle dish?
8. Describe Ethan's "retreat."
9. What does Mattie's note to Ethan say?
10. Why does Ethan think of the man from the other side of the mountain?
11. Why does Ethan's farm have no value as a source of alimony?
12. Ethan intends to manipulate Mr. Hale into giving Ethan the money he owes for the lumber. What changes Ethan's mind?

Assignment 7
Chapter 9 & Epilogue
1. Why is Mattie sitting on her trunk sobbing?
2. What order does Ethan give Mattie after Zeena tells her to hurry up?
3. Why is Daniel Byrne at Ethan's house?
4. What reason does Zeena give that Jotham should drive Mattie to the train station?
5. At the church picnic, what lost item did Ethan find in the moss?
6. What "illusion" does Ethan have by the pond?
7. What object does Mattie announce to Ethan that she'd found?
8. What has Mattie been wishing "every minute of every day"?
9. What does Mattie tell Ethan they can do so they will never have to leave each other?
10. Why does the sled swerve when Ethan and Mattie are headed toward the elm?
11. What are the narrator's observations about the kitchen when he arrives at the Frome household with Ethan?
12. What does Mrs. Hale say about Zeena's thoughts?
13. What, according to Mrs. Hale, was a miracle?
14. Whom does Mrs. Hale believe has suffered most from the "accident"?
15. What about the "accident" does Mrs. Hale say is a pity?
16. To whom does Mrs. Hale compare Ethan, Zeena, and Mattie?

STUDY GUIDE QUESTIONS ANSWER KEY *Ethan Frome*

Assignment 1
<u>Prologue and Chapter 1</u>

1. In what city is the story set?
   The story is set in Starkfield, Massachusetts.
2. Why does the narrator consider Ethan the most striking figure in Starkfield?
   Ethan has a careless, powerful look, in spite of his lameness.
3. What does Zeena often receive in the mail?
   Zeena often receives patent medicine in the mail.
4. What is Zeena's real name?
   Zeena's real name is Zenobia.
5. Why hasn't Ethan moved away from Starkfield?
   Ethan has had sick relatives to care for and couldn't move after his "smash-up."
6. Why is the narrator in Starkfield?
   The narrator was sent by his employers on a job related to building a power-house.
7. The narrator lodges with Mrs. Ned Hale. What is he hoping to learn from her?
   He is hoping Mrs. Hale will tell him all about Ethan and his life.
8. What service does Ethan provide for the narrator?
   The narrator finds himself in need of transportation to Cordury Flats and hires Ethan to drive him.
9. For what reason does Ethan offer the narrator lodging?
   The snow and cold have made the ride to Mrs. Hale's place too dangerous.
10. What caused a premature end to Ethan's studies?
    The death of his father and the misfortunes following it put a premature end to Ethan's studies.
11. Why does Ethan sneak up and look in the church window?
    He has come to town to walk Mattie home, and he is watching her dance with Denis Eady.
12. What color is Mattie's scarf?
    Mattie's scarf is "cherry-colored" or red.
13. Why is Mattie living with Ethan and Zeena?
    Mattie is Zenna's cousin, and she is there to help Zeena.
14. For what reason does Zeena say Mattie will discontinue her services?
    Zeena says Mattie's services will cease when she gets married to someone like Denis Eady.
15. What does Zeena say causes Ethan to be late?
    Zeena says that taking time to shave every day causes Ethan's lateness.
16. How does Ethan feel toward Denis Eady?
    Ethan is jealous of Denis Eady.

Assignment 2
Chapter 2
1. What does Denis offer Mattie outside of the church?
   Denis offers to take Mattie for a ride in his father's cutter, but Mattie refuses.
2. What is "coasting"?
   Coasting is sledding.
3. What happened to Ruth Varnum and Ned Hale while coasting?
   They came very close to hitting the big elm at the bottom of the coasting hill and were nearly killed.
4. When Ethan tells Mattie that people say it is natural for her to leave Ethan and Zeena, what is Mattie's response?
   Mattie asks Ethan if that is what people say or if it is really that Zeena is unhappy with her.
5. What does Ethan imagine is written on every tombstone in the family plot?
   "We never got away--how should you?"
6. What does Ethan fantasize about Mattie while passing through the graveyard?
   Ethan fantasizes that they will always be together on the farm and that she will be buried next to him there.
7. What is different when Ethan and Mattie arrive home from the church dance?
   The key that Zeena usually left under the kitchen door mat is not there.
8. What surprises Ethan when Zeena opens the door to let him and Mattie in after the dance?
   Ethan is surprised by his wife's appearance. He feels as if he had never before known what his wife looked like.
9. Why does Ethan say he has mill accounts to go over?
   Ethan does not want Mattie to see him follow Zeena up to bed, so he uses the mill accounts as an excuse to stay downstairs.

Assignment 3
Chapter 3
1. With specific memory preoccupies Ethan on the morning after the dance at the church?
   Ethan is preoccupied with the memory of Mattie's shoulder against his.
2. In what business had Mattie's father been engaged?
   Mattie's father was in the "drug" or pharmacy business.
3. How did Mattie obtain $50 after her parents left her impoverished?
   She sold her piano.
4. What about Zeena's appearance startles Ethan when he returns from hauling wood?
   She is wearing her best dress.
5. Why does Zeena travel to Bettsbridge?
   Zeena travels to Bettsbridge to consult with a doctor.
6. Ethan tells Zeena he can not take her to the train in Corbury Flats because he has to collect money from Mr. Hale for the lumber. Why does he regret this lie?
   Ethan regrets telling the lie not only because it is untrue but also because he knows from experience it is not good for Zeena to know Ethan has money before she leaves to see the doctor.

Assignment 4
Chapter 4

1. How does Zeena's absence affect the appearance of the kitchen?
   The kitchen appears more homelike.
2. On what did Ethan and Zeena agree when they were married?
   They would sell the farm and saw mill and move to a large town.
3. What reason does Zeena give for becoming quiet like Ethan's mother?
   She says Ethan never listens.
4. Why does Hale ask for an extension to pay his bill?
   He is building a house for Ned and Ruth.
5. What is different about Mattie's hair when Ethan arrives home from Hale's stable?
   She has added a red ribbon.
6. What does the cat knock off the table and break?
   The cat breaks Zeena's special, red, pickle dish, which Zeena never used.

Assignment 5
Chapters 5 & 6

1. What is the only "drawback" to Ethan's contentment while sitting in the kitchen with Mattie?
   He can not see Mattie from his seat.
2. How does Ethan react when he sees Mattie in Zeena's chair?
   He is momentarily shocked.
3. What had Ethan and Mattie previously planned to do the night the pickle dish was broken?
   They had planned to go coasting.
4. What topic of conversation does Ethan decide is vulgar after he brings it up?
   Ethan decides that the topic of Ned and Ruth's kissing is vulgar.
5. About what does Mattie worry while sewing next to Ethan?
   Mattie worries that Zeena has something against her.
6. What does Mattie do when Ethan kisses the material she is sewing?
   Mattie slides it from his hand, rolls it up, and leaves the table.
7. What does Ethan remember when Mattie goes up to bed?
   Ethan remembers that he had not even touched Mattie's hand.
8. Who is Jotham Powell?
   Jotham Powell is Ethan's occasional employee.
9. What does Ethan want to say to Mattie with "his heart in his throat"?
   "We will never be alone like this again."
10. What happens to one of the mares on the way to the wood lot?
    It slips on ice and injures its knee.
11. Why does Ethan go to Michael Eady's place?
    Ethan goes to Michael Eady's place to purchase glue to repair the pickle dish.
12. What surprise does Ethan receive when he returns home from Michael Eady's place?
    Zeena has already arrived home and is up in her room.
13. What is Ethan's reaction to Jotham's refusal to stay for supper?
    Ethan feels there is something ominous in his refusal.

Assignment 6
<u>Chapters 7 & 8</u>
1. What does Ethan initially think when Zeena remarks that she is very ill?
   He hopes it is true.
2. What is Dr. Buck's suggestion for Zeena?
   Dr. Buck suggests that Zeena should hire a girl because Zeena should not do a single thing around the house.
3. According to Zeena, what caused her to lose her health?
   Zeena says that caring for Ethan's mother caused her to lose her health.
4. Ethan tells Zeena she is the wife of a poor man and they can not afford the girl she has hired. How does Zeena react?
   Zeena tells Ethan that there will be more money without Mattie's board expenses, then she laughs.
5. What causes Ethan's sense of helplessness at the end of his and Zeena's conversation concerning Mattie?
   Ethan realizes that Zeena is never going to change her mind.
6. What does Zeena discover while looking for her stomach powders?
   Zeena discovers the broken red pickle dish.
7. What reason does Mattie give for using the pickle dish?
   She wanted to make the supper table pretty.
8. Describe Ethan's "retreat."
   It is a study that is roughly furnished; he hoped to create a scholarly office, but it is an unrefined and cold place.
9. What does Mattie's note to Ethan say?
   "Don't trouble, Ethan."
10. Why does Ethan think of the man from the other side of the mountain?
    The man left his wife. She divorced him and sold their farm, then she invested the farm proceeds into a restaurant. The man and his lover married and had a child. Everyone was happy. Ethan wished he could do something like that.
11. Why does Ethan's farm have no value as a source of alimony?
    It is mortgaged to the limit of its value.
12. Ethan intends to manipulate Mr. Hale into giving Ethan the money he owes for the lumber. What changes Ethan's mind?
    Ethan runs into Mrs. Hale while on his way to see Mr. Hale, and she is very kind to him. Ethan realizes he would be taking the money under false pretenses, and he does not want to take advantage of the Hales.

Assignment 7
<u>Chapter 9 & Epilogue</u>
1. Why is Mattie sitting on her trunk sobbing?
   It is the day she is to leave Zeena and Ethan's home. She is crying because she thinks she might never see Ethan again.
2. What order does Ethan give Mattie after Zeena tells her to hurry up?
   Ethan tells Mattie to let go of her trunk.
3. Why is Daniel Byrne at Ethan's house?
   Daniel Byrne has come to take Mattie's trunk to the station.
4. What reason does Zeena give that Jotham should drive Mattie to the train station?
   She wants Ethan to fix the stove in Mattie's room.

5. At the church picnic, what lost item did Ethan find in the moss?
   Ethan found Mattie's gold locket.
6. What "illusion" does Ethan have by the pond?
   Ethan has an illusion that he is free to marry and is wooing Mattie, the girl he meant to marry.
7. What object does Mattie announce to Ethan that she'd found?
   Mattie announces that she'd found Ethan's letter to Zeena.
8. What has Mattie been wishing "every minute of every day"?
   She has been wishing that she were dead.
9. What does Mattie tell Ethan they can do so they will never have to leave each other?
   She suggests that they run straight into the big elm and kill themselves.
10. Why does the sled swerve when Ethan and Mattie are headed toward the elm?
    Ethan sees Zeena's face and tries to brush it aside. His motion causes the sled to swerve.
11. What are the narrator's observations about the kitchen when he arrives at the Frome household with Ethan?
    It is cold and poorly-appointed; it is worthy of shame and embarrassment.
12. What does Mrs. Hale say about Zeena's thoughts?
    No one knows them.
13. What, according to Mrs. Hale, was a miracle?
    Zeena's ability to care for others despite her illnesses was a miracle.
14. Whom does Mrs. Hale believe has suffered most from the "accident"?
    She believes Ethan has suffered most.
15. What about the "accident" does Mrs. Hale say is a pity?
    Mrs. Hale says the fact that Mattie lived after the accident is a pity.
16. To whom does Mrs. Hale compare Ethan, Zeena, and Mattie?
    She compares them to "the Fromes in the graveyard," saying the two groups are no different.

MULTIPLE CHOICE STUDY/QUIZ QUESTIONS
Ethan Frome

Assignment 1
Prologue and Chapter 1

1. In what city is the story set?
    A. Snowvale, Massachusetts
    B. Boston, Massachusetts
    C. Andover, Massachusetts
    D. Starkfield, Massachusetts

2. Why does the narrator consider Ethan the most striking figure in Starkfiled?
    A. Ethan has oxen-like forearms.
    B. Ethan has stunningly dark hair.
    C. Ethan has a careless, powerful look.
    D. Ethan has a robust figure.

3. What does Zeena often receive in the mail?
    A. Patent medicine
    B. Catalogs for seeds
    C. Letters from her cousin Alexis
    D. Letters from Mattie

4. What is Zeena's real name?
    A. Zemirah
    B. Zephrine
    C. Zenobia
    D. Zinnia

5. Why hadn't Ethan moved away from Starkfield?
    A. Ethan had sick relatives to care for.
    B. Ethan thought the landscape was too beautiful to leave it behind.
    C. He was unable to get into college.
    D. His fiancee did not want to leave.

6. Why is the narrator in Starkfield?
    A. The narrator was sent by his employers on a job related to building a power-house.
    B. The narrator was sent by his employers on a job related to building a railroad.
    C. The narrator was sent by his employers on a job related to building a saw-mill.
    D. The narrator was sent by his employers on a job related to breeding horses.

7. The narrator lodges with Mrs. Ned Hale, what is he hoping to learn from her?
    A. He is hoping Mrs. Hale will tell him where her husband hides his money.
    B. He is hoping Mrs. Hale will tell him all about Zeena and her life.
    C. He is hoping Mrs. Hale will tell him all about Mattie's father.
    D. He is hoping Mrs. Hale will tell him all about Ethan and his life.

8. What service does Ethan provide for the narrator?
    A. He boards and exercises the narrator's horses.
    B. He manages a saw-mill.
    C. He chops firewood.
    D. He provides the narrator with transportation.

9. For what reason does Ethan offer the narrator lodging?
    A. The snow and cold have made the ride too dangerous.
    B. Jotham cannot provide lodging.
    C. The narrator's inn burns down.
    D. Ethan's wife is eager for company.

10. What caused a premature end to Ethan's studies?
    A. His heart was broken by Ruth.
    B. The death of his father
    C. He realized that he wanted to run the saw-mill.
    D. Zeena's pregnancy

11. Why does Ethan sneak up and look in the church window?
    A. He has come to bring Mattie home, and he is watching her dance with Denis Eady.
    B. He has come to town for the dance, but he is afraid to go in.
    C. He is watching Mattie dance with Jotham.
    D. He has come to bring Zeena home, and he is watching her dance with Denis Eady.

12. What color is Mattie's scarf?
    A. White as snow
    B. Robin's egg blue
    C. Cherry-colored
    D. Silvery like the moon

13. Why is Mattie living with Ethan and Zeena?
    A. Mattie is Zenna's cousin, and she is there to help take care of Ethan.
    B. Mattie is Ethan's cousin, and she is there to help Zeena.
    C. Mattie is Zenna's cousin, and she is there to help keep the books at the saw-mill.
    D. Mattie is Zenna's cousin, and she is there to help Zeena.

14. For what reason does Zeena say Mattie will discontinue her services?
    A. Mattie will leave when she gets married to someone like Denis Eady.
    B. Mattie will leave when has enough money to go to Boston.
    C. Mattie will leave when she gets a better job.
    D. Mattie will leave when her mother's health becomes worse then Zeena's.

15. What does Zeena say causes Ethan to be late?
    A. Daydreaming
    B. Taking time to shave every day
    C. Going to bed too late
    D. Walking at night

16. How does Ethan feel toward Denis Eady?
    A. Ethan is jealous of Denis Eady.
    B. Ethan thinks he is a terrific husband for Mattie.
    C. Ethan thinks he is unfair in business.
    D. Ethan admires him deeply.

Assignment 2
Chapter 2

1. What does Denis offer Mattie outside of the church?
    A. He offers to build her a sleigh.
    B. He offers to take her out to a show.
    C. He offers his advice.
    D. He offers her a ride in his father's cutter.

2. What is "coasting"?
    A. Ice skating
    B. Skiing
    C. Sledding
    D. Dancing

3. What happened to Ruth Varnum and Ned Hale while coasting?
    A. Ruth and Ned were killed.
    B. Ruth and Ned were almost killed.
    C. Ruth was killed, and Ned was crippled.
    D. Ned was killed, and Ruth was crippled.

4. When Ethan tells Mattie that people say it is natural for her to leave Ethan and Zeena, what is Mattie's reponse?
    A. Mattie wants to know if that is what people say or if it is really that Zeena is unhappy with her.
    B. Mattie is relieved.
    C. Mattie tells Ethan people should mind their own business.
    D. Mattie wants to know if that is what people say or if it is really that Ethan is unhappy with her.

5. What does Ethan imagine is written on every tombstone in the family plot?
    A. "We never got away--how should you?"
    B. "We never got away--you should"
    C. "Ethan and Zeena until death"
    D. "Run away"

6. What does Ethan fantasize about Mattie while passing through the graveyard?
    A. They will run away and get married.
    B. They will get married on the hill.
    C. They will go coasting, and Mattie will not be afraid because Ethan is with her.
    D. They will always be together, and she will be buried next to him.

7. What is different when Ethan and Mattie arrive home from the church dance?
    A. Zeena is waiting for them on the porch.
    B. The kitchen door is unlocked.
    C. There is light coming from Zeena's room.
    D. The key is not under the kitchen mat.

8. What surprises Ethan when Zeena opens the door to let himself and Mattie in after the dance?
    A. Ethan is surprised by his wife's appearence.
    B. Ethan is surprised by his wife's new robe.
    C. Ethan is surprised when the cat runs out the door.
    D. Zeena has made a fresh pot of tea for Ethan and Mattie.

9. Why does Ethan say he has mill accounts to go over?
    A. He needs to wait downstairs for Mattie.
    B. He doesn't want Mattie to see him follow Zeena up to bed.
    C. He is going to leave Zeena, and he wants go while she is sleeping.
    D. He is angry with Zeena, and he knows she hates to go to bed alone.

Assignment 3
Chapter 3

1. What specific memory proccupies Ethan the morning after the dance at the church?
    A. The smell of Mattie's hair
    B. Mattie's shoulder against his
    C. The glitter of the stars
    D. His wedding day

2. In what business had Mattie's father been engaged?
    A. Dairy farming
    B. Drug/pharmacy
    C. Selling pianos
    D. Milling wood

3. How did Mattie obtain $50 after her parents left her impoverished?
    A. She sold baked goods.
    B. She sold her piano.
    C. She sold her hats.
    D. She sold her gold ring.

4. What about Zeena's appearance startles Ethan when he returns from hauling wood?
    A. She is wearing clothes for a funeral.
    B. She is wearing Mattie's scarf.
    C. She is wearing her best dress.
    D. She is wearing makeup.

5. Why does Zeena travel to Bettsbridge?
    A. To consult with a doctor
    B. To test Ethan's fidelity
    C. To buy goods for the farm
    D. To have an operation

6. Ethan tells Zeena he can not take her to the train in Corbury Flats because he has to collect money from Mr. Hale for the lumber. Why does he regret this lie?
    A. He will have to give the money to Zeena before she leaves.
    B. He knows that Zeena will learn the truth when she talks to Mrs. Hale.
    C. Zeena is going to Bettsbridge and will buy new clothes.
    D. Zeena is going to see the doctor and may spend more money than they actually have.

Assignment 4
Chapter 4

1. How does Zeena's absence affect the appearance of the kitchen?
    A. It is lonely without her.
    B. The kitchen appears more homelike.
    C. It seems cleaner.
    D. It is dark.

2. On what did Ethan and Zeena agree when they were married?
    A. They would have two children.
    B. They would put an addition on the house.
    C. They would sell the farm and saw-mill and move to a large town.
    D. Ethan would care for Zeena's illnesses.

3. What reason does Zeena give for becoming quiet like Ethan's mother?
    A. She says she lacks company.
    B. She says Ethan never listens.
    C. She says Ethan is intellectually below her.
    D. She has gone insane due to lonely farm life.

4. Why does Hale ask for an extension to pay his bill?
    A. His wife spends too much money.
    B. He has significant gambling debts.
    C. He is building a house for Ned and Ruth.
    D. No one wants to build homes.

5. What is different about Mattie's hair when Ethan arrives home from Hale's stable?
    A. She has covered it with a kerchief.
    B. She left it down for Ethan to admire.
    C. She has styled it the same as Zeena's.
    D. She has added a red ribbon.

6. What does the cat knock off the table and break?
    A. Ethan's pipe
    B. Zeena's pickle dish
    C. Mattie's gold locket
    D. Zeena's salt and pepper shakers

Assignment 5
Chapters 5 & 6

1. What is the only "drawback" to Ethan's contentment while sitting in the kitchen with Mattie?
    A. He can not see Mattie from his seat.
    B. He is sweating profusely.
    C. He is hungry because he had not eaten anything.
    D. He can not stop thinking of Zeena.

2. How does Ethan react when he sees Mattie in Zeena's chair?
    A. He is momentarily shocked.
    B. He feels an unbridled passion for Mattie.
    C. He feels judged by Zeena.
    D. He is afraid for a moment.

3. What had Ethan and Mattie previously planned to do the night the pickle dish was broken?
    A. Walk to a dance
    B. Clean the kitchen
    C. Go coasting/sledding
    D. Drive to the train station

4. What topic of conversation does Ethan decide is vulgar after he brings it up?
    A. Jotham's kissing Ruth
    B. Denis's kissing Ruth
    C. Ned's kissing Ruth
    D. Zeena's health

5. About what does Mattie worry while sewing next to Ethan?
    A. Mattie worries that she will not get the sewing done.
    B. Mattie worries that Jotham will kiss her.
    C. Mattie worries that Zeena has something against her.
    D. Mattie worries that Denis Eady will propose.

6. What does Mattie do when Ethan kisses the material she is sewing?
    A. She kisses on the same spot that Ethan had kissed it.
    B. She kisses Ethan's hand.
    C. She slides it from his hand, rolls it up, and leaves the table.
    D. She slides it from his hand, folds it, and gives it to Ethan.

7. What does Ethan remember when Matie goes up to bed?
   A. Ethan remembers that Zeena is waiting at the train station.
   B. Ethan remembers that the cows must be fed.
   C. Ethan remembers that he had not even touched Mattie's hand.
   D. Ethan remembers seeing Mattie with the red ribbon in her hair.

8. Who is Jotham Powell?
   A. Zeena's brother
   B. Mattie's prospective husband
   C. Store owner
   D. Ethan's occasional employee

9. What does Ethan want to say to Mattie with "his heart in his throat"?
   A. "Put your head on my shoulder."
   B. "Do not marry Denis Eady."
   C. "We will never be alone like this again."
   D. "Thank you."

10. What happens to one of the mares on the way to the wood lot?
    A. Ethan is forced to sell it.
    B. It slips on ice and injures its knee.
    C. It slips on ice and breaks a leg.
    D. It is bitten by a snake and dies.

11. Why does Ethan go to Michael Eady's place?
    A. To confront Denis Eady
    B. To sell his mare
    C. To purchase a new pickle dish
    D. To purchase glue

12. What surprise does Ethan receive when he returns home from Michael Eady's place?
    A. Mattie has died.
    B. Zeena has dies.
    C. Zeena is home.
    D. Mattie has run away.

13. What is Ethan's reaction to Jotham's refusal to stay for supper?
    A. Ethan is relieved because he wants to be alone with Mattie.
    B. Ethan is relieved because he knows Zeena does not like Jotham.
    C. Ethan feels there is something ominous in his refusal.
    D. Ethan is angry and tells Jotham he will never be asked to stay again.

Assignment 6
Chapters 7 & 8

1. What does Ethan initially think when Zeena remarks that she is very ill?
    A. He hopes it is true.
    B. He recalls how much he loved Zeena.
    C. He hopes it is not true.
    D. He remembers his mother's pain.

2. What is Dr. Buck's suggestion for Zeena?
    A. To have an operation
    B. To move to a warmer climate
    C. To move to Bettsbridge
    D. To hire a girl as a servant

3. According to Zeena, what caused her to lose her health?
    A. Living in the city
    B. Her husband's infidelities
    C. Caring for Ethan's mother
    D. Having to do farm chores

4. Ethan tells Zeena she is the wife of a poor man, and they can not afford the girl she has hired. How does Zeena react?
    A. Zeena is very angry and tells Ethan she will have help even if he has to work day and night.
    B. Zeena slaps Ethan and goes to her room to cry.
    C. Zeena agrees with Ethan and apologizes for her selfishness.
    D. Zeena tells Ethan that there will be more money without Mattie's board expenses, and then she laughs.

5. What realization causes Ethan's sense of helplessness after his conversation with Zeena concerning Mattie?
    A. Mattie is a terrible housekeeper.
    B. Zeena will live forever.
    C. Zeena is never going to change her mind.
    D. Ethan will always be trapped in Starkfield.

6. What does Zeena discover while looking for her stomach powders?
   A. Love letters
   B. Ethan's train tickets
   C. Fifty dollars
   D. The broken red pickle dish

7. What reason does Mattie give for using the pickle dish?
   A. She wanted to hurt Zeena.
   B. She wanted to make the supper table pretty.
   C. She felt life on the farm was too ordinary.
   D. She found it in the kitchen.

8. Describe Ethan's "retreat."
   A. It is his imagination.
   B. It is a crude horse stall.
   C. It is a beautifully-appointed library.
   D. It is a study that is roughly furnished.

9. What does Mattie's note to Ethan say?
   A. "I love you."
   B. "Please help me."
   C. "Come away with me."
   D. "Don't trouble, Ethan."

10. Why does Ethan think of the man from the other side of the mountain?
    A. Ethan knows the man is happy because he married a woman he loved.
    B. The man left his wife and married his lover; his wife sold their farm to invest into a restaurant, so everyone was happy.
    C. The man has always lived alone and Ethan thinks that is a good way to live.
    D. The man's life fell apart when he left his wife for another woman.

11. Why does Ethan's farm have no value as alimony?
    A. The land is leased from a landlord.
    B. It is poor land, and crops do not grow.
    C. It is mortgaged to the limit of its value.
    D. Zeena is already the owner of the land.

12. Ethan intends to manipulate Mr. Hale into giving Ethan the money he owes for the lumber. What changes Ethan's mind?
    A. Because of Mr. Hale's kindness he realizes he can not take advantage of the Hales.
    B. Because of Mrs. Hale's kindness he realizes he can not take advantage of the Hales.
    C. Ethan decides to steal the money from Denis Eady instead.
    D. He is too embarrassed to ask the Hales for money.

Assignment 7
Chapter 9 & Epilogue

1. Why is Mattie sitting on her trunk sobbing?
   A. Ethan has just told her she has to leave.
   B. Zeena has just told her she has to leave.
   C. She is leaving and realizes she might never see Ethan again.
   D. She is leaving and can not find her red scarf.

2. What order does Ethan give Mattie after Zeena tells her to hurry up?
   A. To kiss him
   B. To give him the letter
   C. To let go of her trunk
   D. To poison Zeena

3. Why is Daniel Byrne at the house?
   A. To bring Mattie to her new job
   B. To take Zeena for her operation
   C. To negotiate a price for the farm
   D. To deliver Mattie's trunk to the station

4. What reason does Zeena give that Jotham should drive Mattie to the train station?
   A. She wants Ethan to be punished.
   B. She wants Ethan to fix the stove in Mattie's room.
   C. She wants Ethan to rub her feet.
   D. She wants to have time alone with Ethan.

5. At the church picnic, what lost item does Ethan find in the moss?
   A. Zeena's calico bonnet
   B. Mattie's gold locket
   C. Mattie's red ribbon
   D. Zeena's gold locket

6. What "illusion" does Ethan have by the pond?
   A. He is free to marry and is wooing Mattie, the girl he meant to marry.
   B. He is going west by train.
   C. This has all been a dream.
   D. He is rich and can afford a divorce.

7. What does Mattie tell Ethan that she had found?
   A. Her missing silver brooch
   B. Ethan's letter to Zeena
   C. Zeena's false teeth
   D. The repaired pickle dish

8. What has Mattie been wishing "every minute of every day"?
   A. She has been wishing that she were dead.
   B. She has been wishing that Denis Eady would propose.
   C. She has been wishing that she had a job as a teacher.
   D. She has been wishing that it would snow.

9. What does Mattie tell Ethan they can do so they will never have to leave each other?
   A. They should kill themselves.
   B. They should go to the train station and run away together.
   C. They should poison Zeena.
   D. They should steal money from Andrew Hale.

10. Why does the sled swerve when Ethan and Mattie are headed toward the elm?
    A. Strong, brutal winds across the hills cause the sled to swerve.
    B. Mattie gets afraid and jumps off the sled, causing it to swerve.
    C. Ethan sees Zeena's face and tries to brush it aside. His motion causes the sled to swerve.
    D. The hand of fate intervenes.

11. What are the narrator's observations about the kitchen when he arrives at the Frome household with Ethan?
    A. It is too warm.
    B. It is cold and poorly-appointed.
    C. It is comforting and welcoming.
    D. It is the heart of the home.

12. What does Mrs. Hale say about Zeena's thoughts?
    A. They are bitter and conniving.
    B. They are evil and menacing.
    C. No one knows them.
    D. Zeena is not in control of them.

13. What, according to Mrs. Hale, is a miracle?
    A. It is a miracle that Mattie and Ethan survived the crash.
    B. Zeena's ability to care for others despite her illnesses is a miracle.
    C. Mattie's ability to care for others despite her injury is a miracle.
    D. Ethan's ability to care for others despite his injury is a miracle.

14. Whom does Mrs. Hale believe has suffered most from the "accident"?
    A. Jotham
    B. Ethan
    C. Zeena
    D. Mattie

15. What about the "accident" does Mrs. Hale say is a pity?
    A. Mattie died.
    B. Mattie became crippled.
    C. Mattie lived.
    D. Mattie became bitter.

16. To whom does Mrs. Hale compare Ethan, Zeena, and Mattie?
    A. The Fromes in the graveyard
    B. Adam and Eve
    C. The ill-fated lovers, Romeo and Juliet
    D. Those who suffered in the Civil War

ANSWER KEY: STUDY QUESTIONS *Ethan Frome*

	1	2	3	4	5	6	7
1	D	D	B	B	A	A	C
2	C	C	B	C	A	D	C
3	A	B	B	B	C	C	D
4	C	A	C	C	C	D	B
5	A	A	A	D	C	C	B
6	A	D	D	B	C	D	A
7	D	D			C	B	B
8	D	A			D	D	A
9	A	B			C	D	A
10	B				B	B	C
11	A				D	C	B
12	C				C	B	C
13	D				C		B
14	A						B
15	B						C
16	A						A

VOCABULARY WORKSHEETS

VOCABULARY ASSIGNMENT 1 *Ethan Frome*

Part I: Using Prior Knowledge and Contextual Clues

Below are the sentences in which the vocabulary words appear in the text. Read the sentence. Use any clues you can find in the sentence combined with your prior knowledge, and write what you think the underlined words mean on the lines provided.

1. Every one in Starkfield knew him and gave him a greeting tempered to his own grave mien; but his taciturnity was respected and it was only on rare occasions that one of the older men of the place detained him for a word.

   _____

2. Every one in Starkfield knew him and gave him a greeting tempered to his own grave mien; but his taciturnity was respected and it was only on rare occasions that one of the older men of the place detained him for a word.

   _____

3. Harmon chuckled sardonically.

   _____

4. Such tastes and acquirements in a man of his condition made the contrast more poignant between his outer situation and his inner needs, ...

   _____

5. At our next meeting he made no allusion to the book, and our intercourse seemed fated to remain as negative and one-sided as if there had been no break in his reserve.

   _____

6. It looked exanimate enough, with its idle wheel looming above the black stream dashed with yellow-white spume, and its cluster of sheds sagging under their white load.

   _____

7. The effect produced on Frome was rather of a complete absence of atmosphere, as though nothing less tenuous than ether intervened between the white earth under his feet and the metallic dome overhead.

   _____

8. Denis Eady was the son of Michael Eady, the ambitious Irish grocer, whose suppleness and effrontery had given Starkfield its first notion of "smart" business methods, and whose new brick store testified to the success of the attempt.

   _____

9. ... he had inwardly demurred at having to do the extra two miles to the village and back after his hard day on the farm; ....

   _____

10. ... but not long afterward he had reached the point of wishing that Starkfield might give all its nights to revelry.

    _____

11. He even noticed two or three gestures which, in his <u>fatuity</u>, he had thought she kept for him ....

_____

Ethan Frome Vocabulary Worksheet Assignment 1 Continued

Part II: Determining the Meaning -- Match the vocabulary words to their dictionary definitions.

____ 1. MIEN   A. Mockingly

____ 2. TACITURNITY   B. Having few words to say

____ 3. SARDONICALLY   C. Demeanor; manner

____ 4. POIGNANT   D. Boldness

____ 5. INTERCOURSE   E. Celebration

____ 6. EXANIMATE   F. Lifeless

____ 7. INTERVENED   G. Communications

____ 8. EFFRONTERY   H. Foolishness

____ 9. DEMURRED   I. Came between disputing people; interceded; mediated OR occurred or existed between two things

____ 10. REVELRY   J. Keenly distressing to the emotions

____ 11. FATUITY   K. Raised doubts or objections

VOCABULARY ASSIGNMENT 2 *Ethan Frome*

Part I: Using Prior Knowledge and Contextual Clues

Below are the sentences in which the vocabulary words appear in the text. Read the sentence. Use any clues you can find in the sentence combined with your prior knowledge, and write what you think the underlined words mean on the lines provided.

1. Frome heard the girl's voice, gaily incredulous: "What on earth's your father's cutter doin' down there?"

   _____

2. By this time they had passed beyond Frome's earshot and he could only follow the shadowy pantomime of their silhouettes as they continued to move along the crest of the slope above him.

   _____

3. The other [arm] he [Eady] tried to slip through hers; but she eluded him nimbly, and Frome's heart, which had swung out over a black void, trembled back to safety.

   _____

4. The other he tried to slip through hers; but she eluded him nimbly ...

   _____

5. "Oh, Ned ain't much at steering. I guess I can take you down all right!" he said disdainfully.

   _____

6. She turned on him with a sudden flash of indignation. "You'd ought to tell me, Ethan Frome--you'd ought to! Unless you want me to go too--"

   _____

7. The answer sent a pang through him but the tone suffused him with joy.

   _____

8. "I guess we'll never let you go, Matt," he whispered, as though even the dead, lovers once, must conspire with him to keep her ....

   _____

9. "Maybe she's forgotten it," Mattie said in a tremulous whisper; but both of them knew that it was not like Zeena to forget.

   _____

Ethan Frome Vocabulary Worksheet Assignment 2 Continued

Part II: Determining the Meaning -- Match the vocabulary words to their dictionary definitions.

____ 1.   INCREDULOUS   A.   Skeptical; unbelieving

____ 2.   PANTOMIME   B.   Spread through

____ 3.   ELUDED   C.   Anger due to injustice

____ 4.   NIMBLY   D.   Play or entertainment in which the performers express themselves only by gestures, without speech

____ 5.   DISDAINFULLY   E.   Avoided; escaped

____ 6.   INDIGNATION   F.   With contempt

____ 7.   SUFFUSED   G.   Jointly make secret plans to commit an unlawful or harmful act

____ 8.   CONSPIRE   H.   Quickly

____ 9.   TREMULOUS   I.   Characterized by trembling, as from fear, nervousness, or weakness

VOCABULARY ASSIGNMENT 3 *Ethan Frome*

Part I: Using Prior Knowledge and Contextual Clues

Below are the sentences in which the vocabulary words appear in the text. Read the sentence. Use any clues you can find in the sentence combined with your prior knowledge, and write what you think the underlined words mean on the lines provided.

1. The sunrise burned red in a pure sky, the shadows on the rim of the wood-lot were darkly blue, and beyond the white and <u>scintillating</u> fields patches of far-off forest hung like smoke.

2. Zeena took the view that Mattie was bound to make the best of Starkfield since she hadn't any other place to go; but this did not strike Ethan as <u>conclusive</u>.

3. Her nearest relations had been <u>induced</u> to place their savings in her father's hands, ...

4. But when Zenobia's doctor recommended her looking about for someone to help her with the house-work the clan instantly saw the chance of exacting a <u>compensation</u> from Mattie.

5. ... Zeena, with more leisure to devote to her complex ailments, grew less watchful of the girl's <u>omissions</u> ....

6. It was formed of Zeena's <u>obstinate</u> silence, or Mattie's sudden look of warning ....

7. In spite of her sedentary habits such abrupt decisions were not without <u>precedent</u> in Zeena's history. Twice or thrice before she had suddenly packed Ethan's valise and started off to Bettesbridge ....

8. ... her husband had grown to dread these <u>expeditions</u> because of their cost.

9. On the brink of departure she was always seized with a <u>flux</u> of words.

10. ... at first he could not think of a <u>pretext</u> for not doing so ....

Ethan Frome Vocabulary Worksheet Assignment 3 Continued

Part II: Determining the Meaning -- Match the vocabulary words to their dictionary definitions.

____ 1. SCINTILLATING   A. Dazzling

____ 2. CONCLUSIVE   B. Journies undertaken with a purpose

____ 3. INDUCED   C. Serving to settle or decide a question; decisive; convincing

____ 4. COMPENSATION   D. Things left out or undone

____ 5. OMISSIONS   E. Act, decision, or case that serves as a guide or justification for subsequent situations

____ 6. OBSTINATE   F. Flow

____ 7. PRECEDENT   G. Excuse put forward to conceal a true purpose or object

____ 8. EXPEDITIONS   H. Moved by persuasion or influence

____ 9. FLUX   I. Stubborn

____ 10. PRETEXT   J. Something given or received as an equivalent for services, debt, loss, injury, suffering, lack, etc.

VOCABULARY ASSIGNMENT 4 *Ethan Frome*

Part I: Using Prior Knowledge and Contextual Clues
Below are the sentences in which the vocabulary words appear in the text. Read the sentence. Use any clues you can find in the sentence combined with your prior knowledge, and write what you think the underlined words mean on the lines provided.

1. At Worcester, ... , he had secretly gloried in being clapped on the back and hailed as "Old Ethe" or "Old Stiff"; and the <u>cessation</u> of such familiarities had increased the chill of his return to Starkfield.

   _____

2. Left alone, after his father's accident, to carry the burden of farm and mill, he had had no time for <u>convivial</u> loiterings in the village ....

   _____

3. After the mortal silence of his long imprisonment Zeena's <u>volubility</u> was music in his ears.

   _____

4. And within a year of their marriage she developed the "sickliness" which had since made her notable even in a community rich in <u>pathological</u> instances.

   _____

5. At times, looking at Zeena's shut face, he felt the chill of such forebodings. At other times her silence seemed deliberately assumed to conceal far-reaching intentions, mysterious conclusions drawn from suspicions and resentments impossible to guess. That <u>supposition</u> was even more disturbing than the other ...

   _____

6. Only one thing weighed on him, and that was his having told Zeena that he was to receive cash for the lumber. He foresaw so clearly the consequences of this <u>imprudence</u> that with considerable reluctance he decided to ask Andrew Hale for a small advance on his load.

   _____

7. ... but his scrupulously clean shirt was fastened by a diamond stud. This display of <u>opulence</u> was misleading, for ... his easygoing habits and the demands of his large family frequently kept him what Starkfield called "behind."

   _____

8. Mattie seemed to feel the <u>contagion</u> of his embarrassment ...

   _____

9. ... he <u>feigned</u> an insatiable appetite for doughnuts and sweet pickles ...

   _____

10. If he glued it together the next morning months might <u>elapse</u> before his wife noticed what had happened ....

    _____

Ethan Frome Vocabulary Worksheet Assignment 4 Continued

Part II: Determining the Meaning -- Match the vocabulary words to their dictionary definitions.

____ 1. CESSATION   A. Wealth; riches

____ 2. CONVIVIAL   B. Act lacking careful consideration or caution

____ 3. VOLUBILITY   C. Hypothesis; theory

____ 4. PATHOLOGICAL   D. Pretended

____ 5. SUPPOSITION   E. Talkativeness

____ 6. IMPRUDENCE   F. Pass, in reference to time

____ 7. OPULENCE   G. Transmission or spread of an idea, emotion, or disease from person to person

____ 8. CONTAGION   H. Sociable

____ 9. FEIGNED   I. Relating to diseases or abnormal health

____ 10. ELAPSE   J. Temporary or complete stopping

VOCABULARY ASSIGNMENT 5 *Ethan Frome*

Part I: Using Prior Knowledge and Contextual Clues
Below are the sentences in which the vocabulary words appear in the text. Read the sentence. Use any clues you can find in the sentence combined with your prior knowledge, and write what you think the underlined words mean on the lines provided.

1. ... but he was too <u>indolent</u> to move and after a moment he said: "Come over here and sit by the stove."

   _____

2. It was almost as if the other face, the face of the <u>superseded</u> woman, had obliterated that of the intruder.

   _____

3. "... I saw a friend of yours getting kissed." ... Ethan had imagined that his <u>allusion</u> might open the way to the accepted pleasantries, and these perhaps in turn to a harmless caress, if only a mere touch on her hand.

   _____

4. The cat had jumped from Zeena's chair to dart at a mouse in the wainscot, and as a result of the sudden movement the empty chair had set up a <u>spectral</u> rocking.

   _____

5. She looked up at him <u>languidly</u>, as though her lids were weighted with sleep and it cost her an effort to raise them.

   _____

6. He remembered afterward, with a grim flash of self-<u>derision</u>, what importance he had attached to the weighing of these probabilities ...

   _____

7. The barn was empty when the horses turned into it and, after giving them the most <u>perfunctory</u> ministrations they had ever received from him, he strode up to the house and pushed open the kitchen door.

   _____

8. He gazed blankly about the kitchen, which looked cold and <u>squalid</u> in the rainy winter twilight.

   _____

9. But the hired man, though seldom <u>loth</u> to accept a meal not included in his wages, opened his stiff jaws to answer slowly: "I'm obliged to you, but I guess I'll go along back."

   _____

10. To Ethan there was something vaguely ominous in this <u>stolid</u> rejection of free food and warmth, and he wondered what had happened on the drive to nerve Jotham to such stoicism.

    _____

Ethan Frome Vocabulary Worksheet Assignment 5 Continued

Part II: Determining the Meaning -- Match the vocabulary words to their dictionary definitions.

____ 1. INDOLENT   A. Lazy

____ 2. SUPERSEDED   B. Ghostly

____ 3. ALLUSION   C. Reluctant; unwilling

____ 4. SPECTRAL   D. Replaced

____ 5. LANGUIDLY   E. Slowly; lacking spirit or liveliness

____ 6. DERISION   F. Casual reference

____ 7. PERFUNCTORY   G. Hasty and superficial

____ 8. SQUALID   H. Foul and repulsive, as from lack of care or cleanliness

____ 9. LOTH   I. Mocking

____ 10. STOLID   J. Without emotion

VOCABULARY ASSIGNMENT 6 *Ethan Frome*

Part I: Using Prior Knowledge and Contextual Clues

Below are the sentences in which the vocabulary words appear in the text. Read the sentence. Use any clues you can find in the sentence combined with your prior knowledge, and write what you think the underlined words mean on the lines provided.

1. It was the <u>consecrated</u> formula, and he expected it to be followed, as usual, by her rising and going down to supper.

   _____

2. But she remained seated, and he could think of nothing more <u>felicitous</u> than: "I presume you're tired after the long ride."

   _____

3. ... he saw in her expedition to Bettsbridge only a plot hatched between herself and her Pierce relations to <u>foist</u> on him the cost of a servant ....

   _____

4. It was the sense of his helplessness that sharpened his <u>antipathy</u>.

   _____

5. Her look smote him with <u>compunction</u>, and he cried out ... "You can't go, Matt! I'll never let you!"

   _____

6. Here he had nailed up shelves for his books, built himself a box-sofa ..., laid out his papers on a kitchen table, hung ... an engraving of Abraham Lincoln and a calendar ..., and tried, with these <u>meagre</u> properties, to produce some likeness to the study of a "minister" who had been kind to him ....

   _____

7. "Don't you take notice when you do [see her]." With this <u>injunction</u> he left her and went out to the cow-barn.

   _____

8. "I'd like to go over things with you first," Zeena continued in an <u>unperturbed</u> voice.

   _____

9. Ethan signed to them to stop, and Mrs. Hale leaned forward, her pink wrinkles twinkling with <u>benevolence</u>.

   _____

Ethan Frome Vocabulary Worksheet Assignment 6 Continued

Part II: Determining the Meaning -- Match the vocabulary words to their dictionary definitions.

____ 1. CONSECRATED   A. Well-suited for the occasion, as an action, manner, or expression; appropriate

____ 2. FELICITOUS   B. Command

____ 3. FOIST   C. Force or impose upon fraudulently or unjustifiably

____ 4. ANTIPATHY   D. Goodwill; kindness

____ 5. COMPUNCTION   E. Deficient in quantity or quality

____ 6. MEAGRE   F. Free from emotional agitation or nervous tension

____ 7. INJUNCTION   G. Guilty uneasiness

____ 8. UNPERTURBED   H. Natural dislike or aversion

____ 9. BENEVOLENCE   I. Sacred

VOCABULARY ASSIGNMENT 7 *Ethan Frome*

Part I: Using Prior Knowledge and Contextual Clues

Below are the sentences in which the vocabulary words appear in the text. Read the sentence. Use any clues you can find in the sentence combined with your prior knowledge, and write what you think the underlined words mean on the lines provided.

1. "That girl that's coming told me she was used to a house where they had a furnace," Zeena persisted with the same <u>monotonous</u> mildness.

   _____

2. They had never before avowed their <u>inclination</u> so openly ...

   _____

3. "Tell me, Matt! Tell me!" he <u>adjured</u> her.

   _____

4. "I could go down this coast with my eyes tied!" and she laughed with him, as if she liked his <u>audacity</u>.

   _____

5. The <u>querulous</u> drone ceased as I entered Frome's kitchen, and of the two women sitting there I could not tell which had been the speaker.

   _____

6. She had pale opaque eyes which revealed nothing and reflected nothing, and her narrow lips were of the same <u>sallow</u> colour as her face.

   _____

7. Beneath their wondering exclamations I felt a secret curiosity to know what impressions I had received from my night in the Frome household, and <u>divined</u> that the best way of breaking down their reserve was to let them try to penetrate mine.

   _____

8. Old Mrs. Varnum, by this time, had gone up to bed, and her daughter and I were sitting alone, after supper, in the <u>austere</u> seclusion of the horse-hair parlour.

   _____

Ethan Frome Vocabulary Worksheet Assignment 7 Continued

Part II: Determining the Meaning -- Match the vocabulary words to their dictionary definitions.

____ 1. MONOTONOUS   A. Guessed using intuition or insight

____ 2. INCLINATION   B. Arrogant boldness or daring

____ 3. ADJURED   C. Sickly, yellowish color

____ 4. AUDACITY   D. Tendency

____ 5. QUERULOUS   E. Requested earnestly or solemnly

____ 6. SALLOW   F. Severely simple; without ornament; lacking softness

____ 7. DIVINED   G. Complaining

____ 8. AUSTERE   H. Lacking in variety; tediously unvarying

VOCABULARY ANSWER KEY - *Ethan Frome*

	1	2	3	4	5	6	7
1	C	A	A	J	A	I	H
2	B	D	C	H	D	A	D
3	A	E	H	E	F	C	E
4	J	H	J	I	B	H	B
5	G	F	D	C	E	G	G
6	F	C	I	B	I	E	C
7	I	B	E	A	G	B	A
8	D	G	B	G	H	F	F
9	K	I	F	D	C	D	
10	E		G	F	J		
11	H						

DAILY LESSONS

LESSON ONE

Objectives
1. To introduce the *Ethan Frome* unit through close observation and creative writing
2. To distribute books and other related materials
3. To preview the study questions for the Prologue and Chapter 1
4. To familiarize students with the vocabulary for the Prologue and Chapter 1
5. To read the Prologue and Chapter 1

Activity 1
This activity asks students to "judge a book by its cover" by observing a photograph of a stranger. This will place students in the same position of the narrator/observer in the story.

Prior to this class period, gather photographs of models of all types from magazines. Students should not be able to identify the model (it should not be a photograph of a celebrity or well-known person). You can instead ask students to bring 2-3 of these pictures. Collect the pictures and then redistribute them so students receive new pictures.

Ask students to take out paper and pens. They will be writing the biography of the person in the picture. Instruct students to write 3-5 paragraphs that provide details about the individual pictured-- students should make up these details such as name, place of birth, occupation, etc. Tell students that some single incident dramatically affected the individual, and that they need to decide what that incident was: did the person win the lottery, get bitten by a shark, become a double agent, get fired from a job?

When students complete the assignment, which should take 15-20 minutes, ask for volunteers to share what they have written and to discuss how and what they observed in the photographs helped them develop their ideas about the characters' biographies.

Activity 2
Distribute the materials students will use in this unit. Explain in detail how students are to use these materials.

Study Guides Students should read the study guide questions for each reading assignment prior to beginning the rading assignment to get a feeling for what events and ideas are important in the section they are about to read. After reading the section, students will (as a class or individually) answer the questions to review the important things from that section of the book. **Review the study questions for the first reading assignment together in class so students can see how to do it.**

Vocabulary Prior to each reading assignment, students will do vocabulary work related to the section of the book they are about to read. Following the completion of the reading of the book, there will be a review of all the words used in the vocabulary assignments. **Do the vocabulary worksheet for the first reading assignment together in class to show students how the worksheets are to be done.**

Reading Assignment Sheet You need to fill in the reading assignment sheets with the appropriate dates. You can either post the schedule where students can easily see it or make copies for each student.

Extra Activities Center The Unit Resource Materials portion of this LitPlan contains suggestions for an extra library of related books and articles in your classroom as well as crossword and word search puzzles. Make an extra activities center in your room where you will keep these materials for students to use. Bring the books and articles in from the library and keep several copies of the puzzles on hand. Explain to students that these materials are available for students to use when they finish reading assignments or other class work early.

Non-fiction Assignment Sheet Explain to students that they each are to read at least one non-fiction piece from the in-class library at some time during the unit. Students will fill out a Non-fiction Assignment Sheet after completing the reading to help you (the teacher) evaluate their reading experiences and to help the students think about and evaluate their own reading experiences.

Books Each school has its own rules and regulations regarding student use of school books. Advise students of the procedures that are normal for your school.

Activity 3
If time allows, begin reading aloud. Emphasize the role of the unnamed narrator. Remind students that the story is framed by this narrator. Tell students that they should annotate as they read, and pay special attention to the narrator's interior thoughts.

If you do not finish the first reading assignment in class, students should do so prior to your next class period.

LESSON TWO

Objectives
1. To review the main ideas and events of the Prologue and Chapter 1
2. To write a factual and informative piece
3. To learn and practice using literary terms
4. To preview the study questions for Chapter 2
5. To do the vocabulary worksheet and reading for Chapter 2

Activity 1
Give students a few minutes to formulate answers for the study guide questions for the Prologue and Chapter 1, and then discuss the answers to the questions in detail. Write the answers on the board or overhead transparency so students can have the correct answers for study purposes.

While students have their study guides out, preview the questions for Chapter 2.

NOTE: It is a good practice in public speaking and leadership skills for individual students to take charge of leading the discussions of the study questions. Perhaps a different student could go to the front of the class and lead the discussion each day that the study questions are discussed in this unit. Of course, you should guide the discussion when appropriate and try to fill in any gaps students may leave. The study questions could be handled in a number of different ways, including in small groups with group reports following. Occasionally you may want to use the multiple choice questions as quizzes to check students' reading comprehension. As a short review now and then, students could pair up for the first (or last, if you have time left at the end of a class period) few minutes of class to quiz each other from the study questions. Mix up the methods of reviewing the materials and checking comprehension throughout the unit so students don't get bored just answering the questions the same way each day. Variety in methods will also help address the different learning styles of your students. From now on in this unit, the directions will simply say, "Discuss the answers to the study questions in detail as previously directed." You will choose the method of preparation and discussion each day based on what best suits your and your class.

Activity 2
Distribute Writing Assignment #1 and discuss the directions in detail. If you use a textbook that defines the literary terms for the assignment, you might plan for students to look up the definitions during class and ask questions if they are unclear. Be sure to give students a due date for turning in this writing assignment.

Activity 3
Students will consider the role of the narrator and the kind of bias that the narrator imposes on the reader. Ask students to take out a sheet of paper and to quickly jot down the story of *Little Red Riding Hood.* Ask students to select a character from the story (the wolf, grandmother, the girl, the woodsman) and to rewrite the story from that character's perspective. Ask students to share their accounts and ask them to consider how the accounts differ between the characters. Now, ask your students to rewrite the story from the perspective of the director of the Fairy Tale Wolf Endangered Species Preserve. How might the story differ then?

Activity 4
Tell students that prior to the next class period they should complete the vocabulary worksheet and read Chapter 2. If time remains in this class, students should work on this assignment.

WRITING ASSIGNMENT #1

PROMPT
To become an expert at writing about literature, one must learn the vocabulary of literature study. Your assignment is to investigate the meanings of three terms from the list below and to write an essay that explains the terms, gives examples, and advises students about how to determine examples in other works of fiction.

allegory	figurative language	omniscient narrator
alliteration	foil	paradox
antagonist	foreshadowing	personification
archetype	flashback	poetic justice
connotation	genre	point of view
denotation	hyperbole	protagonist
denouement	image	rising action
diction	irony	setting
didactic	mood	symbol
exposition	motif	theme
falling action	narrator	tone

PREWRITING
Begin by selecting 4-5 possible terms from the list. Using a textbook, a packet provided by your teacher, or the Internet, look up the definitions of each of these terms. If you use the Internet, be sure to evaluate the credibility of the web sites you use. Carefully write down the definitions and make note of the sources that you used. Now you must think of examples from books or films with which you are familiar for your terms. Thinking of examples will help you determine which three terms will be included in your essay. If you have trouble thinking of an example for one term, you might eliminate that term. Once you have thought of an example, think about how you know that specific example fits the definition of the term. For example, how do you know that Spiderman is a protagonist?

DRAFTING
Write an introductory paragraph which explains why students should be familiar with the terms you selected to define. In the body of your composition, write one paragraph for each of the terms you are presenting. In each paragraph, begin by defining the term, then offer your example(s) and explanations as to how the example fits the definition. Write a concluding paragraph in which you remind readers how to identify these literary elements in stories.

PROMPT
When you finish the rough draft of your composition, ask a student whose opinions you trust to read it. After reading your rough draft, he/she should tell you what he/she liked best about your work, which parts were difficult to understand, and ways in which your work could be improved.

PROOFREADING
Reread your paper considering your critic's comments, and make the corrections you think are necessary. Do a final proofreading of your paper, double-checking your grammar, spelling, organization, and the clarity of your ideas.

WRITING EVALUATION FORM - *Ethan Frome*

Name _____ Date _____

Grade _____

Circle One For Each Item:

Grammar: correct errors noted on paper

Spelling: correct errors noted on paper

Punctuation: correct errors noted on paper

Legibility: excellent   good   fair   poor

_____   excellent   good   fair   poor

_____   excellent   good   fair   poor

Strengths:

Weaknesses:

Comments/Suggestions:

LESSON THREE

<u>Objectives</u>
1. To review the main ideas and events of Chapter 2
2. To review the vocabulary for Chapter 2
3. To assess students' oral reading skills
4. To practice recognizing subtext and inferencing about characters while reading
5. To preview the study questions for Chapter 3
6. To do the voacbulary worksheet and reading for Chapter 3

<u>Activity 1</u>
Discuss the answers to the study questions for Chapter 2 as previously directed. While students have their study guides out, preview the questions for Chapter 3.

<u>Activity 2</u>
Review the answers to the vocabulary for Chapter 2. Post the answers so studends will have the correct answers for study purposes.

<u>Activity 3</u>
Use a portion of this class to work on recognizing inferences.

Have students consider this passage from Chapter 2:

In the black shade of the Varnum spruces he caught up with her and she turned with a quick, "Oh!" ...

"Then you meant to walk home all alone?"
"Oh, I ain't afraid!" she laughed....

"The elm is dangerous, though. It ought to be cut down," she insisted.
"Would you be afraid of it, with me?"
"I told you I ain't the kind to be afraid," she tossed back, almost indifferently; and
 suddenly she began to walk on with a rapid step.

Ask students, "Was Mattie afraid?" After getting responses, ask, "How do you
know that she was?" Dissect the exact words and phrases that imply she was afraid.

Then consider this passage:

"You ain't crying are you, Matt?"
"No, of course I'm not," she quavered.

Ask students, "Was Mattie crying? She says she isn't." After getting student
responses, point out the author's choice of the word "quavered." Discuss what that
single word does in the passage.

Discuss the last page and a half of Chapter 2, beginning with "She walked out of the kitchen ahead of them and pausing in the hall raised the lamp at arm's-length, as if to light them up the stairs."

What do the characters say? What do they actually mean? How do you know what is really going on underneath the visible action?

Discuss ways to find clues as to the underlying meaning of passages.

If time permits, continue practicing making inferences about characters. Ask students to write down the three major characters (Zeena, Ethan, and Mattie) on a piece of paper, leaving space. Give the students these directions: imagine that each character will be granted three wishes. Write down what you think each character might wish and why. For example, would Mattie wish for money, a husband, or for Zeena to disappear? Give students about ten minutes to complete the assignment and share student responses. Note: this activity can also be completed in groups.

<u>Activity 4</u>
Tell students that prior to the next class period they should complete the vocabulary worksheet and reading for Chapter 3.

LESSON FOUR

<u>Objectives</u>
1. To review the main ideas and events of Chapter 3
2. To review the vocabulary for Chapter 3
3. To assess student learning
4. To practice and assess student oral reading
5. To preview the study questions for Chapter 4
6. To do the vocabulary worksheet and reading for Chapter 4

<u>Activity 1</u>
Discuss the answers to the study questions for Chapter 3 as previously directed. While students have their study guides out, preview the questions for Chapter 4.

<u>Activity 2</u>
Review the answers to the vocabulary for Chapter 3. Post the answers so studends will have the correct answers for study purposes.

<u>Activity 3</u>
To review the chapter quickly, have each student select one of the major characters (Zeena, Ethan, or Mattie). Ask students to freewrite 1-2 paragraphs about what they perceive is their character's greatest fear. Ask students to share their discoveries with the group. As you wind up the discussion, challenge students to think about how fear works, and why fear may or may not dominate the thoughts of these characters. In other words: of what are these characters so afraid?

<u>Activity 4</u>
Have students read Chapter 4 of *Ethan Frome* aloud in class. You probably know the best way to get readers with your class; pick students at random, ask for volunteers, or use whatever method works best for your group. If you have not yet completed an oral reading evaluation for your students this period, this would be a good opportunity to do so. A form is included with this unit for your convenience.

<u>Activity 5</u>
Tell students that prior to the next class period they should completed the vocabulary worksheet and reading for Chapter 4.

ORAL READING EVALUATION - *Ethan Frome*

Name _____ Class _____ Date _____

SKILL	EXCELLENT	GOOD	AVERAGE	FAIR	POOR
Fluency	5	4	3	2	1
Clarity	5	4	3	2	1
Audibility	5	4	3	2	1
Pronunciation	5	4	3	2	1
	5	4	3	2	1
	5	4	3	2	1

Total   Grade

Comments:

LESSON FIVE

Objectives
1. To review the main ideas and events of Chapter 4
2. To review the vocabulary for Chapter 4
3. To assess student learning
4. To practice creative analytical writing
5. To preview the study questions Chapters 5 and 6
6. To do the vocabulary worksheet and reading for Chapters 5 and 6

Activity 1
Discuss the answers to the study questions for Chapter 4 as previously directed. While students have their study guides out, preview the questions for Chapters 5 and 6.

Activity 2
Review the answers to the vocabulary for Chapter 4. Post the answers so studends will have the correct answers for study purposes.

Activity 3
Ask students to take out their books and review their annotations, focusing on the details about Zeena's initial arrival to Starkfield. Together as a class, list as many details from the text about this earlier time in Zeena's life as possible.

Students will use these details as they assume Zeena's persona and write a 2-3 paragraph diary entry that shows her feelings and attitudes towards her situation and towards Ethan, from the time before she was married to him.

When students have completed the exercise, they can share some or all of their entries. As students share, ask them to consider whether their responses depict Zeena as happy and optimistic, or as controlling and scheming. How does this shape the way readers perceive Zeena? Do we feel sympathy for her? Why or why not?

Activity 4
Tell students that prior to the next class period they should complete the vocabulary worksheet and reading for Chapters 5 and 6. If time remains in this class period, students should begin this assignment.

LESSON SIX

Objectives
1. To review the main ideas and events of Chapters 5 and 6
2. To review the vocabulary for Chapters 5 and 6
3. To consider characterization in an analytical way
4. To practice critical thinking and persuasion
5. To preview the study questions for Chapters 7 and 8
6. To do the vocabulary worksheet and reading for Chapters 7 and 8

Activity 1
Discuss the answers to the study questions for Chapters 5 and 6 as previously directed.

Activity 2
Review the answers to the vocabulary for Chapters 5 and 6. Post the answers so studends will have the correct answers for study purposes.

Activity 3
Today in class you will have a jigsaw activity to facilitate student discussion about Ethan, his thoughts and actions, and his culpability in the situation (which may or may not be an affair).

Break students into four groups with the same number of members. Each group will be assigned one of the following positions:
Ethan Frome is moral.
Ethan Frome is immoral.
Ethan Frome is guilty.
Ethan Frome is not guilty.

Each group should begin by defining the situation: for example, has Ethan committed adultery?

Then, group members should discuss their position and find proof in the story that corroborates their position. Each group should find 2-3 quotes that support their position. Students should make note of these so they can share them with other students later.

Then, regroup students so each position is represented in each group. Ask students to share their findings. When each group member has shared, students in the group must come to consensus over the following questions:
Is Ethan Frome moral or immoral?
Is Ethan Frome guilty or not guilty?

If consensus is not easily reached, students should argue their positions and use their quotes to persuade other group members.

Activity 4
Tell students that prior to the next class period they should complete the vocabulary sheet and reading for Chapters 7 and 8. If time remains in this class period, students should work on this assignment.

LESSON SEVEN

<u>Objectives</u>
1. To review main ideas and events of Chapters 7 and 8
2. To review the vocabulary for Chapters 7 and 8
3. To study text in an analytical way
4. To preview the study questions for Chapter 9 and the Epilogue
5. To do the vocabulary worksheet and reading for Chapter 9 and the Epilogue

<u>Activity 1</u>
Discuss the answers to the study questions for Chapters 7 and 8 as previously directed. While students have their study guides out, preview the questions for Chapter 9 and the Epilogue.

<u>Activity 2</u>
Review the answers to the vocabulary for Chapters 7 and 8. Post the answers so students will have the correct answers for study purposes.

<u>Activity 3</u>
Look carefully at the beginning of Chapter 8, which is the description of Ethan's study. Ask students to annotate the first six paragraphs of the chapter, focusing on the items in the study. As a whole class, identify as many items as possible. List the items on the board. After you have made an exhaustive list, begin to consider why each item is significant. What do the items suggest about Ethan?

Look at the next few paragraphs where Ethan considers different courses of action-- a divorce, running away with Mattie, and so on. How do these options relate to the items in the study?

Now, consider the study itself: how does the study represent Ethan?

Lastly, look at the moment in the chapter when Mattie enters the study. Why is it significant that Mattie enters the study? Keeping this in mind, ask again: how does the study represent Ethan?

<u>Activity 4</u>
Tell students that prior to the next class period they should complete the vocabulary sheet and reading for Chapter 9 and the Epilogue. If time remains in this class period, students should work on this assignment.

LESSON EIGHT

Objectives
1. To review the main ideas and events of Chapter 9 and the Epilogue
2. To review the vocabulary for Chapters 9 and the Epilogue
3. To discuss irony and the conclusion of the story

Activity 1
Discuss the answers to the study questions for Chapter 9 and the Epilogue as previously directed.

Activity 2
Review the answers to the vocabulary for Chapters 9 and the Epilogue. Post the answers so students will have the correct answers for study purposes.

Activity 3
Ask students to freewrite about their responses to the reversal that occurs at the end of the story. Ask students if they guessed the ending, or if the reversal was unexpected.

Then, ask students to look carefully at the descriptions of Zeena and Mattie. Based on the text, how, specifically, have the characters switched places? For example, Zeena is now a caretaker, and Mattie is an invalid.

Share the definition of irony: a literary technique in which contrast or incongruity creates meaning. Ask students if they feel that the ending is ironic: have Zeena and Mattie gotten what they deserve? Why or why not?

LESSON NINE

Objectives
1. To connect the book *Ethan Frome* to real life
2. To expose students to more information about a variety of topics related to the novel

Activity 1

Take students to the library/media center to find articles, books, etc. about non-fiction topics related to *Ethan Frome*. Each student should select a different topic related to the novel.

Some suggested topics are:

Attitudes toward marriage and/or divorce in the early 20th century
America's shift from being an agrarian to industrial nation
Hypochondria and its causes
The decline of the family farm in America
Edith Wharton's life
Depression and loneliness in rural settings
Winter in New England
The role of women in society in the early 20th century
Patent medicine and quackery
Protestant values in New England
Spinal cord injuries
Suicide

Activity 2

Students should complete the Non-fiction Assignment Sheet, answering all questions as thoroughly as possible. Tell students they will be giving an oral report on their non-fiction topic in Lesson Thirteen.

Your criteria for evaluating this report will vary depending on the level of your students. You may have students give a complete report without using notes of any kind, or you may want students to read directly from a written report, or you may want to do something in between those two extrems. Just make students aware of your criteria in ample time for them to prepare their reports.

NON-FICTION ASSIGNMENT SHEET *Ethan Frome*

Name _____ Date _____

Title of Nonfiction Read _____

Written By _____ Publication Date _____

I. Factual Summary: Write a short summary of the piece you read.

II. Vocabulary
1. With which vocabulary words in the piece did you encounter some degree of difficulty?

2. How did you resolve your lack of understanding with these words?

III. Interpretation: What was the main point the author wanted you to get from reading his work?

IV. Criticism
1. With which points of the piece did you agree or find easy to accept? Why?

2. With which points of the piece did you disagree or find difficult to believe? Why?

V. Personal Response: What do you think about this piece? **OR** How does this piece influence your ideas?

LESSON TEN

Objectives
1. To review symbol, motif, and theme
2. To interpret literature collaboratively in a group
3. To identify important passages in *Ethan Frome*

Activity 1
Write the words "symbol," "motif," and "theme" on the board. Ask students to define the terms. A symbol is an object that represents an idea. A motif is a collection of related symbols. A theme is a message which a text conveys.

Activity 2
Break class into small groups. The size of the groups will depend on the size and level of your class. Each group should consider either symbols, motifs, or themes in the novel.

If there are many people in the groups, each member should review a chapter or two of the book with the groups topic in mind, recording any applicable references or ideas that appear in his/her chapter(s).

If there are only a few people in the groups, they should skim through the book together recording any references or ideas that relate to their topic.

After having time to skim and record, students should talk about what they found and write down a list of statements that are their conclusions.

Activity 3
Groups will report their findings to the whole class. Students should refer the class to important passages from the text.

Activity 4
If time permits, ask students to identify which symbol they perceive as the most important and tell why.

LESSON ELEVEN

Objectives
    1. To study themes represented in *Ethan Frome*
    2. To understand conflict
    3. To introduce Writing Assignment #2

Activity 1
Tell your class that you will be focusing on Ethan's character for this class period. Ask students to generate a list of themes and conflicts which mostly affect Ethan. Guide students to "discover" themes and conflicts such as: individual happiness versus responsibility, failure, success, duty, obligation, Zeena versus Mattie, frustration, sacrifice, agency to make choices, and so on.

When you have a list, ask students to consider Ethan's fate: is he culpable or not? Then, have students share their thoughts. Finally, ask students how Ethan could have achieved happiness. Steer their discussion toward goal-setting, i.e. that Ethan might have set goals to achieve his dreams more easily.

Activity 2
Discuss the qualities of good goals. Have students give some examples of goals and work as a class to refine the goals to the best possible forms. For example, a goal might be, "to lose weight." Refine that goal using the "SMART" formula (Specific, Measurable, Achievable, Realistic, Time-Bound). "Lose 5 pounds within the next month by eliminating my morning doughnut and taking a morning walk each day." Do several examples together as a class.

Activity 3
Distribute Writing Assignment #2. Discuss the directions in detail. Tell students they will be completing this assignment in the next class period.

LESSON TWELVE

<u>Objectives</u>
1. To assess student writing
2. To learn to set goals
3. To learn to write about oneself with specificity
4. To practice writing with time limits

<u>Activity</u>
Give students the entire class period to complete Writing Assignment #2.

WRITING ASSIGNMENT 2 *Ethan Frome*

PROMPT
Successful people know that the best way to ensure success is by carefully setting goals. For this assignment, you will write about three goals that you would like to achieve. Additionally, you will write about why you want to achieve these goals. In total, your essay should be 5 to 7 fully-developed paragraphs.

Goals should be written with attention to several points. A goal should be:

S - Specific
M - Measurable
A - Achievable
R - Realistic
T - Time-bound

This means that a goal should be specific, measurable, possible to achieve, realistic in its ambition, and set in a specific time frame. Consider this example: I want to do well in school. A better version would be: I would like to raise my math grade from 82% to 90% by the end of the next marking period by handing in all my homework assignments and earning a B+ or above on all tests.

PREWRITING
Choose three different things you would like to improve. Write a goal for each, then revise your goals using the "SMART" formula. Think about all the areas of your life and how you could set goals to improve these areas: Do you need more sleep? Do you want to earn a raise at your part-time job? Do you want to spend more time with your family?

DRAFTING
Your introductory paragraph should mention your goals briefly and explain your views on how to set goals and why to set goals.

Your body paragraphs should explain one goal each in great detail, explaining the goal itself and the actions you will have to take to achieve it, as well as how you will judge whether or not you have succeeded. Be sure to explain why the goal is important to you.

In your concluding paragraph, summarize your goals and restate why attaining these goals is particularly significant for you.

PROOFREADING
Do a final proofreading of your paper, double-checking your grammar, spelling, organization, and the clarity of your ideas.

LESSON THIRTEEN

<u>Objectives</u>
1. To widen the breadth of students' knowledge about the topics discussed or touched upon in *Ethan Frome*
2. To check students' non-fiction reading assignments

<u>Activity</u>
Ask each student to give a brief oral report about the non-fiction articles he/she read for the unit project assignment.

Start with one student's report. After that, ask if anyone else in the class has read on a topic related to the first student's report. If no one has, choose another student at random. After each report, be sure to ask if anyone has a report related to the one just completed. That will help keep a continuity during the discussion about the information students have just heard.

LESSON FOURTEEN

Objectives

1. To review close reading and passage analysis skills
2. To identify connotations and denotations of words, figures of speech, symbols, motifs, and other literary devices
3. To think beyond identifying important words or phrases to be able to recognize the varying levels of importance of the words and phrases used
4. To identify one key word or phrase and explain its significance in relation to the novel

Activity

Distribute a copy of the Close Passage Analysis to each student and complete in class. Review the directions and expectations for completing close passage analysis in a satisfactory way. As students annotate and write responses, walk around the class to see if any students need individual coaching.

After students have written about their discoveries, share them as a whole class. As you discuss, continuously bring students back to the language of the text and show them how meaning is rooted in individual words.

CLOSE PASSAGE ANALYSIS *Ethan Frome*

Directions: Read the passage below carefully. As you read, pay attention to important words and phrases, circling or underlining them. You should look up the meaning of any words that you do not know. Consider the connotation and denotation of words. Pay special attention to any figures of speech such as similes or metaphors. Additionally, be aware of any symbols or motifs which appear in the passage. If any words or phrases make you think of ideas, jot them in the margin.

Zeena stood beside the ruin of her treasure, stiffening into a stony image of resentment, "You got down my pickle-dish--what for?"

A bright flush flew to Mattie's cheeks. "I wanted to make the supper-table pretty," she said.

"You wanted to make the supper-table pretty; and you waited 'til my back was turned, and took the thing I set most store by of anything I've got, and wouldn't never use it, not even when the minister come to dinner, or Aunt Martha Pierce come over from Bettsbridge--" Zeena paused with a gasp, as if terrified by her own evocation of the sacrilege. "You're a bad girl, Mattie Silver, and I always known it. It's the way your father begun, and I was warned of it when I took you, and I tried to keep my things where you couldn't get at 'em--and now you've took from me the one I cared for most of all--" She broke off in a short spasm of sobs that passed and left her more than ever like a shape of stone.

"If I'd 'a' listened to folks, you'd 'a gone before now, and this wouldn't 'a happened," she said; and gathering up the bits of broken glass she went out of the room as if she carried a dead body...

Review your annotations. Is there one word or phrase which seems the most important? Freewrite 1-2 paragraphs about the significance of your most important discovery.

LESSON FIFTEEN

Objectives
1. To identify the value of the book *Ethan Frome*
2. To practice writing persuasively
3. To evaluate students' writing

Activity

Distribute Writing Assignment #3. Discuss the directions in detail and give students ample time to complete the assignment. Allowing students to begin working on the assignment during this class period. Tell students when the assignment is due.

While students are writing, call individual students to your desk or some other private area for a writing conference based on the first two writing assignments in this unit. An evaluation form is included in this unit for your convenience. Also, review students' annotations of their selected passages to make sure they have rich ideas for exploring in their writing.

WRITING ASSIGNMENT #3 *Ethan Frome*

PROMPT
Ethan Frome was originally published in 1911, yet here we are still reading it so many years later. Why? What is the intrinsic value of this book? What does it offer to readers today? Your assignment is to write a letter to a student in the next class that will have to read *Ethan Frome* and persuade him/her that Ethan Frome isn't just a dusty, old, has-been book; it has important messages for us today.

PREWRITING
What are the messages in Ethan Frome? Jot down some ideas and themes that have been discussed in class--and add some of your own if you can. What did you learn from this book? What did you see in it that was valuable? Jot down notes about those things, too.

Think about how you felt when you were told you had to read this book. How do you think students will feel when they have to read it next week or next month or next year? What could you possibly say to persuade him/her that the book is a worthwhile read? Make notes about your thoughts.

Consider your audience and consider your points. Come up with a plan as to which points are most likely to persuade the student to whom you are writing. Make a little rough outline (and revise it as necessary) to map out your writing plan.

DRAFTING
Write this assignment in the form of a letter. You may pick out a particular student or address it simply to Dear Student. Write an introductory paragraph letting the student know why you are writing. Use several paragraphs in the body of your letter to make your persuasive points and support them, following your outline/map. Write a final paragraph in which you conclude your letter and perhaps give final advice.

PROMPT
When you finish the rough draft of your letter, ask a student whose opinions you trust to read it. After reading your rough draft, he/she should tell you what he/she liked best about your work, which parts were difficult to understand, and ways in which your work could be improved. Reread your paper considering your critic's comments, and make the corrections you think are necessary.

PROOFREADING
Do a final proofreading of your letter, double-checking your grammar, spelling, organization, and the clarity of your ideas.

LESSON SIXTEEN & SEVENTEEN

Objectives
1. To have students think about the conventions of storytelling
2. To introduce a group project
3. To practice creative writing

Activity 1
Ask students to think about the fairy tales that they know, especially *Snow White* and *Cinderella*. Based on what they know, ask them to infer why fairy tales exist. What purpose and function do they serve? Who is the intended audience for fairy tales, and why?

Read your students a brief version of *Snow White* (or, even a different culture's version of the story such as the Scottish story *Silver Tree and Gold Tree*). Ask them to make notes on the similarities they see echoed in *Ethan Frome*. Then, discuss their observations. Is *Ethan Frome* a fairy tale? What elements of the fairy tale does it share? Is the story the exact opposite of what we would expect a fairy tale to be? How can we explain the ending of *Ethan Frome*? Does the story have the same kind of moral element as a fairy tale?

Activity 2
Divide students into groups of 3-4. (You can assign student or allow them to select their groups.) Distribute the Group Assignment Sheet and discuss the directions in detail. Tell students they will have the remainder of this class period and the next to work in their groups. Be sure students know when this assignment is due.

PROJECT ASSIGNMENT *Ethan Frome*

PROMPT
Do you wish *Ethan Frome* had a happier ending? Do you wish that Ethan could be free from obligation or that he would stand up to Zeena? Do you wish Zeena would confront Mattie about Ethan? You will get your wish, as you will work in groups of 3-4 to rewrite moments from *Ethan Frome*.

Each group will select a pivotal moment from the text and create a "Choose Your Own Adventure" alternative. If you recall from when you were younger, these books allowed the reader to select the course of action for the protagonist to take. Basically, you will create a story that has multiple endings, depending on the choices that your character makes. Your "alternatives" should join together to create a truly alternate ending.

REQUIREMENTS
Each group member should write about at least two moments, and all totaled, each group should produce 8-12 pages (typed and double-spaced).

PROMPT
Think hard about the moments you select: perhaps Ethan glues the pickle dish together, maybe Zeena is told she has only weeks to live, or perhaps Mattie accepts a proposal from Denis Eady.

Note: The entire story is available online as an e-text. It may be helpful to cut and paste segments of the story as you write.

It may also be helpful to lay out your "alternatives" in your word processing program so that the paper is the same size as your book, so you can literally slide your new "alternatives" into the place in the book that is most relevant.

LESSON EIGHTEEN

<u>Objectives</u>
To review all of the vocabulary work done in this unit

<u>Activity 1</u>
Choose one (or more) of the vocabulary review activities listed on the next page and spend your class period as directed in the activity. Some of the materials for these review activities are located in the Vocabulary Resource Materials section in this LitPlan.

<u>Activity 2</u>
Ask students to complete another review activity for homework.

VOCABULARY REVIEW ACTIVITIES *Ethan Frome*

1. Divide your class into two teams and have an old-fashioned spelling or definition bee.

2. Give each of your students (or students in groups of two, three, or four) an *Ethan Frome* Vocabulary Word Search Puzzle. The person (group) to find all of the vocabulary words in the puzzle first wins.

3. Give students an *Ethan Frome* Vocabulary Word Search Puzzle without the word list. The person or group to find the most vocabulary words in the puzzle wins.

4. Use an *Ethan Frome* Vocabulary Crossword Puzzle. Put the puzzle onto a transparency on the overhead projector (so everyone can see it), and do the puzzle together in class.

5. Give students an *Ethan Frome* Vocabulary Matching Worksheet to do.

6. Divide your class into two teams. Use *Ethan Frome* vocabulary words with their letters jumbled as a word list. Student 1 from Team A faces off against Student 1 from Team B. You write the first jumbled word on the board. The first student (1A or 1B) to unscramble the word wins the chance for his/her team to score points. If 1A wins the jumble, go to student 2A and give him/her a clue. He/she must give you the correct word which matches that clue. If he/she does, Team A scores a point, and you give student 3A a clue for which you expect another correct response. Continue giving Team A clues until some team member makes an incorrect response. An incorrect response sends the game back to the jumbled word face-off, this time with students 2A and 2B. Instead of repeating giving clues to the first few students of each team, continue with the student after the one who gave the last incorrect response on the team. For example, if Team B wins the jumbled word face-off, and student 5B gave the last incorrect answer for Team B, you would start this round of clue questions with student 6B, and so on. The team with the most points wins!

7. Have students write a story in which they correctly use as many vocabulary words as possible. Have students read their compositions orally! Post the most original compositions on your bulletin board!

8. Adapt a popular board game concept like Taboo! to use in the classroom. For example, students may not say any of the words that are part of the definitions provided in the Vocabulary Worksheets section.

LESSON NINETEEN

Objective
To discuss *Ethan Frome* at an in-depth, analytical level

Activity 1
Students will review material through a jigsaw activity. To make this work, there should be a number of students equal to the number of groups per group (for example, four groups of four students).

Select the appropriate number of questions from the Critical or Critical/Personal sections of the Extra Writing Assignments/Discussion Questions, and assign one to each group. The group should discuss the question, and each member of the group should write a full response to the question.

Then, regroup the students so that each group has a representative from each of the previous groups. Students will take turns sharing the discoveries of their earlier groups.

Activity 2
If time permits, ask students to identify the questions which they believe may be on their test. Discuss these as a whole class.

EXTRA DISCUSSION QUESTIONS *Ethan Frome*

<u>Interpretive</u>
1. Explain how having an unknown and detached narrator affects the reader's perceptions of the characters in *Ethan Frome*.
2. What is the climax of the story?
3. Explain how the setting of a rural community is significant in the story.
4. What is the main conflict in the story?
5. The story has characters with both external and internal conflicts. Does one kind of conflict contribute more significantly to the plot overall?
6. The novel shifts from the first person perspective of the narrator to a limited omniscient perspective. The limited omniscient perspective allows the reader to know only Ethan's deepest thoughts. How does this affect the perceptions of the reader?
7. At several points, Wharton offers foreshadowing of the events that unfold in the story. Identify these moments in the text and explain how they add meaning to the text.

<u>Critical</u>
8. Discuss the functions of the minor characters, especially Mrs. Ned Hale. How do these characters affect the reader's view of the major characters?
9. What, ultimately, is the attitude of the story toward family?
10. Why is the story titled *Ethan Frome*?
11. Does the novel depict a tension between the city and country? What does the city represent for Ethan, Zeena, and Mattie? What does the country represent for them?
12. How are Zeena and Mattie foils for one another?
13. How do imagination and illusion function in the story?
14. What does *Ethan Frome* suggest about marriage and the role of women in society?
15. Explain how the motif of winter is significant in the story.

<u>Critical/Personal Response</u>
16. The story can be interpreted in a way that suggests that characters are served their "just desserts." Does the text suggest that they are responsible for their own fates, or does the text suggest that they are victims?
17. Does this story have a clear antagonist? If so, what is it? If not, what is it that is causing conflict within the story?
18. Is Ethan motivated by true desire or loneliness?
19. What change occurs in Mattie by the end of the story? Was this change surprising?
20. Is Zeena's hypochondria a way to gain attention, love, sympathy, control, or something else?
21. Are the main characters ruled by outside circumstances, or do they have control over their lives?
22. For the major characters, is poverty a result of their attitudes?
23. What causes Ethan to always do the "right" thing? Does he have moral character?
24. Does Zeena know about Ethan's feelings toward Mattie? What evidence is available to support your answer?
25. What makes Zeena angrier: the thought that Ethan loves Mattie or that Mattie loves Ethan?
26. Did his evening alone with Mattie actually meet Ethan's expectations, or was it merely a hopeful delusion?

Personal Response
27. Do you think that Ethan gives in to the pressure to conform?
28. Did you enjoy reading *Ethan Frome*? Why or why not?
29. Did you dislike any characters in *Ethan Frome*? Why?
30. If you were Ethan, would you have run away with Mattie? Why or why not?
31. Do you think Zeena used Ethan and obligated him to marry her? Explain.
32. Do you feel sympathy for Ethan? Pity? Scorn? Why?
33. Did the story's resolution seem obvious? Why or why not?
34. Do you think Mattie and/or Ethan are guilty of adultery? Why or why not?

LESSON TWENTY

<u>Objectives</u>
1. To review the main ideas and events in *Ethan Frome*
2. To learn how to prioritize material for test preparation

<u>Activity 1</u>
Choose one of the review games/activities suggested on the following page and spend your class time as directed there.

<u>Activity 2</u>
Ask students if they have questions about their upcoming test. Advise students how best to prepare for their assessment and which materials they should review.

REVIEW GAMES/ACTIVITIES *Ethan Frome*

1. Ask the class to make up a unit test for *Ethan Frome*. The test should have 4 sections: matching, true/false, short answer, and essay. Students may use 1/2 of the class period to make the test and then swap papers and use the other 1/2 class period to take a test (open book) a classmate has devised. You may want to use the unit test included in this packet or take questions from the students' unit tests to formulate your own test.

2. Take 1/2 of the class period for students to make up true and false questions, including their answers. Collect the papers and divide the class into two teams. Draw a big tic-tac-toe board on the chalk board. Make one team X and one team O. Ask questions to each side, giving each student one turn. If the question is answered correctly, that student's team's letter (X or O) is placed in the box. If the answer is incorrect, no letter is placed in the box. The object is to get three in a row like tic-tac-toe. You may want to keep track of the number of games won for each team.

3. Take 1/2 of the class period for students to make up questions (true/false and short answer). Collect the questions. Divide the class into two teams. You'll alternate asking questions to individual members of teams A & B (like in a spelling bee). The question keeps going from A to B until it is correctly answered, then a new question is asked. A correct answer does not allow the team to get another question. Correct answers are +2 points; incorrect answers are -1 point.

4. Have students pair up and quiz each other from their study guides and class notes.

5. Give students an *Ethan Frome* crossword puzzle to complete.

6. Divide your class into two teams. Use *Ethan Frome* crossword words with their letters jumbled as a word list. Student 1 from Team A faces off against Student 1 from Team B. You write the first jumbled word on the board. The first student (1A or 1B) to unscramble the word wins the chance for his/her team to score points. If 1A wins the jumble, go to student 2A and give him/her a clue. He/she must give you the correct word which matches that clue. If he/she does, Team A scores a point, and you give student 3A a clue for which you expect another correct response. Continue giving Team A clues until some team member makes an incorrect response. An incorrect response sends the game back to the jumbled word face-off, this time with students 2A and 2B. Instead of repeating giving clues to the first few students of each team, continue with the student after the one who gave the last incorrect response on the team. For example, if Team B wins the jumbled word face-off, and student 5B gave the last incorrect answer for Team B, you would start this round of clue questions with student 6B, and so on. The team with the most points wins!

7. Play What's My Line?. This is similar to the old television show. Students assume the roles of different characters from the novel. One student gives clues to the class, or to a panel of contestants. The contestants try to guess the identity of the guest. Students may enjoy assisting you in creating rules and procedures for the game.

8. Play Jeopardy. Divide the class into two groups. Assign each group a category or book from the novel and have them devise answers for that category. Play the game according to the television show procedures.

9. Play Drawing in the Details. This is similar to Pictionary. Divide students into teams. A student from one team draws a scene from the novel. You may want to specify the section. Drawings should be kept simple, to keep the pace lively. Students on the opposing team locate the scene in their books and read it aloud. If they are incorrect, the illustrator's team has a chance to guess. Involve students in setting up a scoring system and any other necessary rules.

LESSON TWENTY

Objectives
To test the students' understanding of the main ideas and themes in *Ethan Frome*

Activity
Distribute the unit tests, give students ample time to complete them, and collect the tests when students finish. Remember to collect assigned books prior to the end of the class period.

NOTES ABOUT THE UNIT TESTS IN THIS UNIT:

There are 5 different unit tests included in the LitPlan Teacher Pack. Two are short answer, two are multiple choice, and there is one advanced short answer test.

The answers to the advanced short answer test will be based on the discussions you have had during class and should be graded accordingly.

You should choose the tests and/or test parts which best suit your needs.

Matching and short answer tests have answer keys. For essay type questions, grade according to your own criteria based on class discussions and the level of your students.

Also, you will need to choose vocabulary words to read orally for the vocabulary section of the short answer tests.

UNIT TESTS

Ethan Frome SHORT ANSWER UNIT TEST 1

I. Matching

____ 1. ZEENA   A. Builds a house as a gift
____ 2. MATTIE   B. He drove the trunk to the station.
____ 3. SILVER   C. Reminder that Ethan will never escape Starkfield
____ 4. STARKFIELD   D. Went insane due to silence
____ 5. NURSE   E. Hired hand
____ 6. DENIS   F. Zeena's destination
____ 7. EADY   G. Left Ruth a widow
____ 8. TOMBSTONE   H. Ethan sees himself as a ___.
____ 9. BETTSBRIDGE   I. Zeena's relative: Aunt _____
____ 10. MOTHER   J. Gave Zeena pickle dish: Aunt ____
____ 11. DISH   K. Surname of Mattie
____ 12. JOTHAM   L. Ethan's houseguest
____ 13. DANIEL   M. Town where Ethan lives
____ 14. RUTH   N. Zeena's first role in the Frome household
____ 15. NED   O. She kissed Ned.
____ 16. HALE   P. Wants to take Mattie on a sleigh ride
____ 17. PRISONER   Q. Object of Ethan's desire
____ 18. MARTHA   R. Mrs. Frome
____ 19. NARRATOR   S. Wealthy family in Starkfield
____ 20. PHILURA   T. It was broken into pieces.

II. Short Answer

1. What does Zeena often receive in the mail?

2. Why hasn't Ethan moved away from Starkfield?

3. For what reason does Zeena say Mattie will discontinue her services?

4. What is "coasting"?

5. What does Ethan imagine is written on every tombstone in the family plot?

6. What does Ethan fantasize about Mattie while passing through the graveyard?

7. In what business had Mattie's father been engaged?

8. Why does Zeena travel to Bettsbridge?

9. How does Zeena's absence affect the appearance of the kitchen?

10. What does Ethan want to say to Mattie with "his heart in his throat"?

11. What does Ethan initially think when Zeena remarks that she is very ill?

12. According to Zeena, what caused her to lose her health?

13. What does Zeena discover while looking for her stomach powders?

14. Describe Ethan's "retreat."

15. Ethan intends to manipulate Mr. Hale into giving Ethan the money he owes for the lumber. What changes Ethan's mind?

16. Why is Mattie sitting on her trunk sobbing?

17. What "illusion" does Ethan have by the pond?

18. Why does the sled swerve when Ethan and Mattie are headed toward the elm?

19. What are the narrator's observations about the kitchen when he arrives at the Frome household with Ethan?

20. What about the "accident" does Mrs. Hale say is a pity?

III. Essays
1. The novel shifts from the first person perspective of the narrator to a limited omniscient perspective. The limited omniscient perspective allows the reader to know only Ethan's deepest thoughts. How does this affect the perceptions of the reader?

IV. Vocabulary
    A. Write the vocabulary words you are given. After writing them down, go back and write in their definitions.

Word	Definition
1	
2	
3	
4	
5	
6	
7	
8	
9	
10	

Ethan Frome SHORT ANSWER UNIT TEST 1 Answer Key

I. Matching

R	1. ZEENA	A.	Builds a house as a gift
Q	2. MATTIE	B.	He drove the trunk to the station.
K	3. SILVER	C.	Reminder that Ethan will never escape Starkfield
M	4. STARKFIELD	D.	Went insane due to silence
N	5. NURSE	E.	Hired hand
P	6. DENIS	F.	Zeena's destination
S	7. EADY	G.	Left Ruth a widow
C	8. TOMBSTONE	H.	Ethan sees himself as a ___.
F	9. BETTSBRIDGE	I.	Zeena's relative: Aunt _____
D	10. MOTHER	J.	Gave Zeena pickle dish: Aunt ____
T	11. DISH	K.	Surname of Mattie
E	12. JOTHAM	L.	Ethan's houseguest
B	13. DANIEL	M.	Town where Ethan lives
O	14. RUTH	N.	Zeena's first role in the Frome household
G	15. NED	O.	She kissed Ned.
A	16. HALE	P.	Wants to take Mattie on a sleigh ride
H	17. PRISONER	Q.	Object of Ethan's desire
I	18. MARTHA	R.	Mrs. Frome
L	19. NARRATOR	S.	Wealthy family in Starkfield
J	20. PHILURA	T.	It was broken into pieces.

II. Short Answer

1. What does Zeena often receive in the mail?
   Zeena often receives patent medicine in the mail.

2. Why hasn't Ethan moved away from Starkfield?
   Ethan has had sick relatives to care for and couldn't move after his "smash-up."

3. For what reason does Zeena say Mattie will discontinue her services?
   Zeena says Mattie's services will cease when she gets married to someone like Denis Eady.

4. What is "coasting"?
   Coasting is sledding.

5. What does Ethan imagine is written on every tombstone in the family plot?
   "We never got away--how should you?"

6. What does Ethan fantasize about Mattie while passing through the graveyard?
   Ethan fantasizes that they will always be together on the farm and that she will be buried next to him there.

7. In what business had Mattie's father been engaged?
   Mattie's father was in the "drug" or pharmacy business.

8. Why does Zeena travel to Bettsbridge?
   Zeena travels to Bettsbridge to consult with a doctor.

9. How does Zeena's absence affect the appearance of the kitchen?
   The kitchen appears more homelike.

10. What does Ethan want to say to Mattie with "his heart in his throat"?
    "We will never be alone like this again."

11. What does Ethan initially think when Zeena remarks that she is very ill?
    He hopes it is true.

12. According to Zeena, what caused her to lose her health?
    Zeena says that caring for Ethan's mother caused her to lose her health.

13. What does Zeena discover while looking for her stomach powders?
    Zeena discovers the broken red pickle dish.

14. Describe Ethan's "retreat."
    It is a study that is roughly furnished; he hoped to create a scholarly office, but it is an unrefined and cold place.

15. Ethan intends to manipulate Mr. Hale into giving Ethan the money he owes for the lumber. What changes Ethan's mind?
    Ethan runs into Mrs. Hale while on his way to see Mr. Hale, and she is very kind to him. Ethan realizes he would be taking the money under false pretenses, and he does not want to take advantage of the Hales.

16. Why is Mattie sitting on her trunk sobbing?
    It is the day she is to leave Zeena and Ethan's home. She is crying because she thinks she might never see Ethan again.

17. What "illusion" does Ethan have by the pond?
    Ethan has an illusion that he is free to marry and is wooing Mattie, the girl he meant to marry.

18. Why does the sled swerve when Ethan and Mattie are headed toward the elm?
    Ethan sees Zeena's face and tries to brush it aside. His motion causes the sled to swerve.

19. What are the narrator's observations about the kitchen when he arrives at the Frome household with Ethan?
    It is cold and poorly-appointed; it is worthy of shame and embarrassment.

20. What about the "accident" does Mrs. Hale say is a pity?
    Mrs. Hale says the fact that Mattie lived after the accident is a pity.

IV. Vocabulary

    Write the vocabulary words and definitions you will use for this test.

Word	Definition
1	
2	
3	
4	
5	
6	
7	
8	
9	
10	

Ethan Frome SHORT ANSWER UNIT TEST 2

I. Matching

____ 1.	ZEENA	A.	Ethan's houseguest
____ 2.	MATTIE	B.	Left Ruth a widow
____ 3.	SILVER	C.	Hired hand
____ 4.	FROME	D.	She kissed Ned.
____ 5.	NURSE	E.	Surname of Ethan
____ 6.	DENIS	F.	Wealthy family in Starkfield
____ 7.	EADY	G.	Zeena's relative: Aunt _____
____ 8.	BETTSBRIDGE	H.	Gave Zeena pickle dish: Aunt _____
____ 9.	MOTHER	I.	Mrs. Frome
____ 10.	JOTHAM	J.	Zeena's destination
____ 11.	SERVANT	K.	Object of Ethan's desire
____ 12.	ILLNESS	L.	Zeena's ability to be a caretaker is this.
____ 13.	DANIEL	M.	Builds a house as a gift
____ 14.	RUTH	N.	Dr. Buck's recommendation for Zeena
____ 15.	NED	O.	Preoccupies Zeena's thoughts
____ 16.	HALE	P.	Went insane due to silence
____ 17.	MIRACLE	Q.	Surname of Mattie
____ 18.	MARTHA	R.	He drove the trunk to the station.
____ 19.	NARRATOR	S.	Zeena's first role in the Frome household
____ 20.	PHILURA	T.	Wants to take Mattie on a sleigh ride

II. Short Answer

1. In what city is the story set?

2. Why is the narrator in Starkfield?

3. What service does Ethan provide for the narrator?

4. Why is Mattie living with Ethan and Zeena?

5. What happened to Ruth Varnum and Ned Hale while coasting?

6. With specific memory preoccupies Ethan on the morning after the dance at the church?

7. In what business had Mattie's father been engaged?

8. Why does Zeena travel to Bettsbridge?

9. What does the cat knock off the table and break?

10. Why does Ethan go to Michael Eady's place?

11. What does Ethan initially think when Zeena remarks that she is very ill?

12. According to Zeena, what caused her to lose her health?

13. Ethan intends to manipulate Mr. Hale into giving Ethan the money he owes for the lumber. What changes Ethan's mind?

14. Why is Mattie sitting on her trunk sobbing?

15. What "illusion" does Ethan have by the pond?

16. What object does Mattie announce to Ethan that she'd found?

17. What has Mattie been wishing "every minute of every day"?

18. What does Mattie tell Ethan they can do so they will never have to leave each other?

19. What are the narrator's observations about the kitchen when he arrives at the Frome household with Ethan?

20. What about the "accident" does Mrs. Hale say is a pity?

III. Essays
1. The story can be interpreted in a way that suggests that characters are served their "just desserts." Does the text suggest that they are responsible for their own fates, or does the text suggest that they are victims?

IV. Vocabulary
> A. Write the vocabulary words you are given. After writing them down, go back and write in their definitions.

Word	Definition
1	
2	
3	
4	
5	
6	
7	
8	
9	
10	

Ethan Frome SHORT ANSWER UNIT TEST 2 Answer Key

I. Matching

I	1.	ZEENA	A.	Ethan's houseguest
K	2.	MATTIE	B.	Left Ruth a widow
Q	3.	SILVER	C.	Hired hand
E	4.	FROME	D.	She kissed Ned.
S	5.	NURSE	E.	Surname of Ethan
T	6.	DENIS	F.	Wealthy family in Starkfield
F	7.	EADY	G.	Zeena's relative: Aunt _____
J	8.	BETTSBRIDGE	H.	Gave Zeena pickle dish: Aunt ____
P	9.	MOTHER	I.	Mrs. Frome
C	10.	JOTHAM	J.	Zeena's destination
N	11.	SERVANT	K.	Object of Ethan's desire
O	12.	ILLNESS	L.	Zeena's ability to be a caretaker is this.
R	13.	DANIEL	M.	Builds a house as a gift
D	14.	RUTH	N.	Dr. Buck's recommendation for Zeena
B	15.	NED	O.	Preoccupies Zeena's thoughts
M	16.	HALE	P.	Went insane due to silence
L	17.	MIRACLE	Q.	Surname of Mattie
G	18.	MARTHA	R.	He drove the trunk to the station.
A	19.	NARRATOR	S.	Zeena's first role in the Frome household
H	20.	PHILURA	T.	Wants to take Mattie on a sleigh ride

II. Short Answer

1. In what city is the story set?
   The story is set in Starkfield, Massachusetts.

2. Why is the narrator in Starkfield?
   The narrator was sent by his employers on a job related to building a power-house.

3. What service does Ethan provide for the narrator?
   The narrator finds himself in need of transportation to Cordury Flats and hires Ethan to drive him.

4. Why is Mattie living with Ethan and Zeena?
   Mattie is Zenna's cousin, and she is there to help Zeena.

5. What happened to Ruth Varnum and Ned Hale while coasting?
   They came very close to hitting the big elm at the bottom of the coasting hill and were nearly killed.

6. With specific memory preoccupies Ethan on the morning after the dance at the church?
   Ethan is preoccupied with the memory of Mattie's shoulder against his.

7. In what business had Mattie's father been engaged?
   Mattie's father was in the "drug" or pharmacy business.

8. Why does Zeena travel to Bettsbridge?
   Zeena travels to Bettsbridge to consult with a doctor.

9. What does the cat knock off the table and break?
   The cat breaks Zeena's special, red, pickle dish, which Zeena never used.

10. Why does Ethan go to Michael Eady's place?
    Ethan goes to Michael Eady's place to purchase glue to repair the pickle dish.

11. What does Ethan initially think when Zeena remarks that she is very ill?
    He hopes it is true.

12. According to Zeena, what caused her to lose her health?
    Zeena says that caring for Ethan's mother caused her to lose her health.

13. Ethan intends to manipulate Mr. Hale into giving Ethan the money he owes for the lumber. What changes Ethan's mind?
    Ethan runs into Mrs. Hale while on his way to see Mr. Hale, and she is very kind to him. Ethan realizes he would be taking the money under false pretenses, and he does not want to take advantage of the Hales.

14. Why is Mattie sitting on her trunk sobbing?
    It is the day she is to leave Zeena and Ethan's home. She is crying because she thinks she might never see Ethan again.

15. What "illusion" does Ethan have by the pond?
    Ethan has an illusion that he is free to marry and is wooing Mattie, the girl he meant to marry.

16. What object does Mattie announce to Ethan that she'd found?
    Mattie announces that she'd found Ethan's letter to Zeena.

17. What has Mattie been wishing "every minute of every day"?
    She has been wishing that she were dead.

18. What does Mattie tell Ethan they can do so they will never have to leave each other?
    She suggests that they run straight into the big elm and kill themselves.

19. What are the narrator's observations about the kitchen when he arrives at the Frome household with Ethan?
    It is cold and poorly-appointed; it is worthy of shame and embarrassment.

20. What about the "accident" does Mrs. Hale say is a pity?
    Mrs. Hale says the fact that Mattie lived after the accident is a pity.

IV. Vocabulary
    Write the vocabulary words and definitions you will use for this test.

Word	Definition
1	
2	
3	
4	
5	
6	
7	
8	
9	
10	

Ethan Frome ADVANCED SHORT ANSWER UNIT TEST 1

I. Matching

____ 1. ZEENA   A. Object of Ethan's desire
____ 2. MATTIE   B. Zeena's first role in the Frome household
____ 3. SILVER   C. Zeena's relative: Aunt _____
____ 4. FROME   D. Gave Zeena pickle dish: Aunt _____
____ 5. STARKFIELD   E. Ethan's academic interest
____ 6. HARMON   F. Surname of Ethan
____ 7. NURSE   G. Ethan's houseguest
____ 8. DENIS   H. Dr. Buck's recommendation for Zeena
____ 9. EADY   I. He drove the trunk to the station.
____ 10. MOTHER   J. Mrs. Frome
____ 11. JOTHAM   K. Surname of Mattie
____ 12. SERVANT   L. Town where Ethan lives
____ 13. DANIEL   M. She kissed Ned.
____ 14. RUTH   N. Wealthy family in Starkfield
____ 15. NED   O. Wants to take Mattie on a sleigh ride
____ 16. PRISONER   P. Went insane due to silence
____ 17. MARTHA   Q. Ethan sees himself as a ___.
____ 18. ENGINEERING   R. Stagecoach driver
____ 19. NARRATOR   S. Hired hand
____ 20. PHILURA   T. Left Ruth a widow

II. Short Answer
1. What is the climax of the story?

2. Explain how the setting of a rural community is significant in the story.

3. Is Ethan motivated by true desire or loneliness?

4. Are the main characters ruled by outside circumstances, or do they have control over their lives?

5. Does Zeena know about Ethan's feelings toward Mattie? What evidence is available to support your answer?

6. What makes Zeena angrier: the thought that Ethan loves Mattie or that Mattie loves Ethan?

7. Explain how the motif of winter is significant in the story.

8. Do you think that Ethan gives in to the pressure to conform?

9. Do you think Zeena used Ethan and obligated him to marry her? Explain.

10. Do you think Mattie and/or Ethan are guilty of adultery? Why or why not?

III. Essays
1. Explain how having an unknown and detached narrator affects the reader's perceptions of the characters in *Ethan Frome*.

2. Discuss the functions of the minor characters, especially Mrs. Ned Hale. How do these characters affect the reader's view of the major characters?

IV. Vocabulary
   A. Write the vocabulary words you are given. After writing them down, go back and write in their definitions.

Word	Definition
1	
2	
3	
4	
5	
6	
7	
8	
9	
10	

B. Write a paragraph about the book using 8 of the 10 vocabulary words above.

Ethan Frome ADVANCED SHORT ANSWER UNIT TEST 1 Answer Key

I. Matching

J	1.	ZENA	A.	Object of Ethan's desire
A	2.	MATTIE	B.	Zeena's first role in the Frome household
K	3.	SILVER	C.	Zeena's relative: Aunt _____
F	4.	FROME	D.	Gave Zeena pickle dish: Aunt _____
L	5.	STARKFIELD	E.	Ethan's academic interest
R	6.	HARMON	F.	Surname of Ethan
B	7.	NURSE	G.	Ethan's houseguest
O	8.	DENIS	H.	Dr. Buck's recommendation for Zeena
N	9.	EADY	I.	He drove the trunk to the station.
P	10.	MOTHER	J.	Mrs. Frome
S	11.	JOTHAM	K.	Surname of Mattie
H	12.	SERVANT	L.	Town where Ethan lives
I	13.	DANIEL	M.	She kissed Ned.
M	14.	RUTH	N.	Wealthy family in Starkfield
T	15.	NED	O.	Wants to take Mattie on a sleigh ride
Q	16.	PRISONER	P.	Went insane due to silence
C	17.	MARTHA	Q.	Ethan sees himself as a ___.
E	18.	ENGINEERING	R.	Stagecoach driver
G	19.	NARRATOR	S.	Hired hand
D	20.	PHILURA	T.	Left Ruth a widow

IV. Vocabulary

Write the vocabulary words and definitions you will use for this test.

Word	Definition
1	
2	
3	
4	
5	
6	
7	
8	
9	
10	

Ethan Frome MULTIPLE CHOICE UNIT TEST 1

I. Matching

____ 1. ZEENA   A. He drove the trunk to the station.
____ 2. MATTIE   B. Mrs. Frome
____ 3. SILVER   C. Left Ruth a widow
____ 4. FROME   D. Surname of Ethan
____ 5. STARKFIELD   E. She kissed Ned.
____ 6. NURSE   F. Wants to take Mattie on a sleigh ride
____ 7. DENIS   G. Object of Ethan's desire
____ 8. EADY   H. Builds a house as a gift
____ 9. TOMBSTONE   I. Reminder that Ethan will never escape Starkfield
____ 10. BETTSBRIDGE   J. Wealthy family in Starkfield
____ 11. MOTHER   K. Hired hand
____ 12. DISH   L. It was broken into pieces.
____ 13. JOTHAM   M. Gave Zeena pickle dish: Aunt ____
____ 14. DANIEL   N. Zeena's first role in the Frome household
____ 15. RUTH   O. Surname of Mattie
____ 16. NED   P. Zeena's relative: Aunt ____
____ 17. HALE   Q. Town where Ethan lives
____ 18. MARTHA   R. Ethan's houseguest
____ 19. NARRATOR   S. Went insane due to silence
____ 20. PHILURA   T. Zeena's destination

II. Multiple Choice

1. What about the "accident" does Mrs. Hale say is a pity?
    A. Mattie became crippled.
    B. Mattie became bitter.
    C. Mattie lived.
    D. Mattie died.

2. What does the cat knock off the table and break?
    A. Ethan's pipe
    B. Zeena's salt and pepper shakers
    C. Zeena's pickle dish
    D. Mattie's gold locket

3. Why does Zeena travel to Bettsbridge?
    A. To consult with a doctor
    B. To test Ethan's fidelity
    C. To have an operation
    D. To buy goods for the farm

4. In what business had Mattie's father been engaged?
    A. Selling pianos
    B. Drug/pharmacy
    C. Milling wood
    D. Dairy farming

5. What does Ethan fantasize about Mattie while passing through the graveyard?
    A. They will go coasting, and Mattie will not be afraid because Ethan is with her.
    B. They will get married on the hill.
    C. They will run away and get married.
    D. They will always be together, and she will be buried next to him.

6. What happened to Ruth Varnum and Ned Hale while coasting?
    A. Ruth was killed, and Ned was crippled.
    B. Ruth and Ned were killed.
    C. Ruth and Ned were almost killed.
    D. Ned was killed, and Ruth was crippled.

7. For what reason does Zeena say Mattie will discontinue her services?
    A. Mattie will leave when she gets married to someone like Denis Eady.
    B. Mattie will leave when has enough money to go to Boston.
    C. Mattie will leave when her mother's health becomes worse then Zeena's.
    D. Mattie will leave when she gets a better job.

8. Why is Mattie living with Ethan and Zeena?
    A. Mattie is Zenna's cousin, and she is there to help Zeena.
    B. Mattie is Zenna's cousin, and she is there to help keep the books at the saw-mill.
    C. Mattie is Ethan's cousin, and she is there to help Zeena.
    D. Mattie is Zenna's cousin, and she is there to help take care of Ethan.

9. Why hadn't Ethan moved away from Starkfield?
    A. Ethan thought the landscape was too beautiful to leave it behind.
    B. He was unable to get into college.
    C. His fiancee did not want to leave.
    D. Ethan had sick relatives to care for.

10. Why does Ethan go to Michael Eady's place?
    A. To purchase glue
    B. To purchase a new pickle dish
    C. To confront Denis Eady
    D. To sell his mare

11. What does Ethan initially think when Zeena remarks that she is very ill?
    A. He hopes it is not true.
    B. He remembers his mother's pain.
    C. He hopes it is true.
    D. He recalls how much he loved Zeena.

12. What are the narrator's observations about the kitchen when he arrives at the Frome household with Ethan?
    A. It is the heart of the home.
    B. It is comforting and welcoming.
    C. It is too warm.
    D. It is cold and poorly-appointed.

13. Why does the sled swerve when Ethan and Mattie are headed toward the elm?
    A. Strong, brutal winds across the hills cause the sled to swerve.
    B. Ethan sees Zeena's face and tries to brush it aside. His motion causes the sled to swerve.
    C. Mattie gets afraid and jumps off the sled, causing it to swerve.
    D. The hand of fate intervenes.

14. What has Mattie been wishing "every minute of every day"?
    A. She has been wishing that it would snow.
    B. She has been wishing that she were dead.
    C. She has been wishing that Denis Eady would propose.
    D. She has been wishing that she had a job as a teacher.

15. What does Mattie tell Ethan that she had found?
    A. Ethan's letter to Zeena
    B. Zeena's false teeth
    C. The repaired pickle dish
    D. Her missing silver brooch

16. What "illusion" does Ethan have by the pond?
    A. He is rich and can afford a divorce.
    B. This has all been a dream.
    C. He is going west by train.
    D. He is free to marry and is wooing Mattie, the girl he meant to marry.

17. Why is Mattie sitting on her trunk sobbing?
    A. She is leaving and can not find her red scarf.
    B. Zeena has just told her she has to leave.
    C. She is leaving and realizes she might never see Ethan again.
    D. Ethan has just told her she has to leave.

18. Ethan intends to manipulate Mr. Hale into giving Ethan the money he owes for the lumber. What changes Ethan's mind?
    A. Because of Mrs. Hale's kindness he realizes he can not take advantage of the Hales.
    B. Ethan decides to steal the money from Denis Eady.
    C. Because of Mr. Hale's kindness he realizes he can not take advantage of the Hales.
    D. He is too embarrassed to ask the Hales for money.

19. According to Zeena, what caused her to lose her health?
    A. Living in the city
    B. Having to do farm chores
    C. Her husband's infidelities
    D. Caring for Ethan's mother

20. What does Zeena often receive in the mail?
    A. Letters from her cousin Alexis
    B. Letters from Mattie
    C. Catalogs for seeds
    D. Patent medicine

III. Essay
1. The story has characters with both external and internal conflicts. Does one kind of conflict contribute more significantly to the plot overall?

IV. Vocabulary

____ 1. POIGNANT   A. Talkativeness
____ 2. INTERCOURSE   B. Transmission or spread of an idea, emotion, or disease from person to person
____ 3. EXANIMATE   C. Keenly distressing to the emotions
____ 4. INTERVENED   D. Celebration
____ 5. EFFRONTERY   E. Communications
____ 6. REVELRY   F. Boldness
____ 7. FATUITY   G. Lifeless
____ 8. PANTOMIME   H. Tendency
____ 9. DISDAINFULLY   I. With contempt
____ 10. OBSTINATE   J. Requested earnestly or solemnly
____ 11. FLUX   K. Without emotion
____ 12. CESSATION   L. Came between disputing people; interceded; mediated OR occurred or existed between two things
____ 13. VOLUBILITY   M. Hypothesis; theory
____ 14. SUPPOSITION   N. Foolishness
____ 15. CONTAGION   O. Play or entertainment in which the performers express themselves only by gestures, without speech
____ 16. INDOLENT   P. Stubborn
____ 17. STOLID   Q. Deficient in quantity or quality
____ 18. MEAGRE   R. Flow
____ 19. INCLINATION   S. Temporary or complete stopping
____ 20. ADJURED   T. Lazy

Ethan Frome MULTIPLE CHOICE UNIT TEST 1 Answer Key

I. Matching

B	1.	ZEENA	A.	He drove the trunk to the station.
G	2.	MATTIE	B.	Mrs. Frome
O	3.	SILVER	C.	Left Ruth a widow
D	4.	FROME	D.	Surname of Ethan
Q	5.	STARKFIELD	E.	She kissed Ned.
N	6.	NURSE	F.	Wants to take Mattie on a sleigh ride
F	7.	DENIS	G.	Object of Ethan's desire
J	8.	EADY	H.	Builds a house as a gift
I	9.	TOMBSTONE	I.	Reminder that Ethan will never escape Starkfield
T	10.	BETTSBRIDGE	J.	Wealthy family in Starkfield
S	11.	MOTHER	K.	Hired hand
L	12.	DISH	L.	It was broken into pieces.
K	13.	JOTHAM	M.	Gave Zeena pickle dish: Aunt ____
A	14.	DANIEL	N.	Zeena's first role in the Frome household
E	15.	RUTH	O.	Surname of Mattie
C	16.	NED	P.	Zeena's relative: Aunt ____
H	17.	HALE	Q.	Town where Ethan lives
P	18.	MARTHA	R.	Ethan's houseguest
R	19.	NARRATOR	S.	Went insane due to silence
M	20.	PHILURA	T.	Zeena's destination

II. Multiple Choice

C 1. What about the "accident" does Mrs. Hale say is a pity?
- A. Mattie became crippled.
- B. Mattie became bitter.
- C. Mattie lived.
- D. Mattie died.

C 2. What does the cat knock off the table and break?
- A. Ethan's pipe
- B. Zeena's salt and pepper shakers
- C. Zeena's pickle dish
- D. Mattie's gold locket

A 3. Why does Zeena travel to Bettsbridge?
- A. To consult with a doctor
- B. To test Ethan's fidelity
- C. To have an operation
- D. To buy goods for the farm

B 4. In what business had Mattie's father been engaged?
- A. Selling pianos
- B. Drug/pharmacy
- C. Milling wood
- D. Dairy farming

D 5. What does Ethan fantasize about Mattie while passing through the graveyard?
- A. They will go coasting, and Mattie will not be afraid because Ethan is with her.
- B. They will get married on the hill.
- C. They will run away and get married.
- D. They will always be together, and she will be buried next to him.

C 6. What happened to Ruth Varnum and Ned Hale while coasting?
- A. Ruth was killed, and Ned was crippled.
- B. Ruth and Ned were killed.
- C. Ruth and Ned were almost killed.
- D. Ned was killed, and Ruth was crippled.

A 7. For what reason does Zeena say Mattie will discontinue her services?
  A. Mattie will leave when she gets married to someone like Denis Eady.
  B. Mattie will leave when has enough money to go to Boston.
  C. Mattie will leave when her mother's health becomes worse then Zeena's.
  D. Mattie will leave when she gets a better job.

A 8. Why is Mattie living with Ethan and Zeena?
  A. Mattie is Zenna's cousin, and she is there to help Zeena.
  B. Mattie is Zenna's cousin, and she is there to help keep the books at the saw-mill.
  C. Mattie is Ethan's cousin, and she is there to help Zeena.
  D. Mattie is Zenna's cousin, and she is there to help take care of Ethan.

D 9. Why hadn't Ethan moved away from Starkfield?
  A. Ethan thought the landscape was too beautiful to leave it behind.
  B. He was unable to get into college.
  C. His fiancee did not want to leave.
  D. Ethan had sick relatives to care for.

A 10. Why does Ethan go to Michael Eady's place?
  A. To purchase glue
  B. To purchase a new pickle dish
  C. To confront Denis Eady
  D. To sell his mare

C 11. What does Ethan initially think when Zeena remarks that she is very ill?
  A. He hopes it is not true.
  B. He remembers his mother's pain.
  C. He hopes it is true.
  D. He recalls how much he loved Zeena.

D 12. What are the narrator's observations about the kitchen when he arrives at the Frome household with Ethan?
  A. It is the heart of the home.
  B. It is comforting and welcoming.
  C. It is too warm.
  D. It is cold and poorly-appointed.

B 13. Why does the sled swerve when Ethan and Mattie are headed toward the elm?
- A. Strong, brutal winds across the hills cause the sled to swerve.
- B. Ethan sees Zeena's face and tries to brush it aside. His motion causes the sled to swerve.
- C. Mattie gets afraid and jumps off the sled, causing it to swerve.
- D. The hand of fate intervenes.

B 14. What has Mattie been wishing "every minute of every day"?
- A. She has been wishing that it would snow.
- B. She has been wishing that she were dead.
- C. She has been wishing that Denis Eady would propose.
- D. She has been wishing that she had a job as a teacher.

A 15. What does Mattie tell Ethan that she had found?
- A. Ethan's letter to Zeena
- B. Zeena's false teeth
- C. The repaired pickle dish
- D. Her missing silver brooch

D 16. What "illusion" does Ethan have by the pond?
- A. He is rich and can afford a divorce.
- B. This has all been a dream.
- C. He is going west by train.
- D. He is free to marry and is wooing Mattie, the girl he meant to marry.

C 17. Why is Mattie sitting on her trunk sobbing?
- A. She is leaving and can not find her red scarf.
- B. Zeena has just told her she has to leave.
- C. She is leaving and realizes she might never see Ethan again.
- D. Ethan has just told her she has to leave.

A 18. Ethan intends to manipulate Mr. Hale into giving Ethan the money he owes for the lumber. What changes Ethan's mind?
- A. Because of Mrs. Hale's kindness he realizes he can not take advantage of the Hales.
- B. Ethan decides to steal the money from Denis Eady.
- C. Because of Mr. Hale's kindness he realizes he can not take advantage of the Hales.
- D. He is too embarrassed to ask the Hales for money.

D 19. According to Zeena, what caused her to lose her health?
   A. Living in the city
   B. Having to do farm chores
   C. Her husband's infidelities
   D. Caring for Ethan's mother

D 20. What does Zeena often receive in the mail?
   A. Letters from her cousin Alexis
   B. Letters from Mattie
   C. Catalogs for seeds
   D. Patent medicine

IV. Vocabulary

C	1.	POIGNANT	A.	Talkativeness
E	2.	INTERCOURSE	B.	Transmission or spread of an idea, emotion, or disease from person to person
G	3.	EXANIMATE	C.	Keenly distressing to the emotions
L	4.	INTERVENED	D.	Celebration
F	5.	EFFRONTERY	E.	Communications
D	6.	REVELRY	F.	Boldness
N	7.	FATUITY	G.	Lifeless
O	8.	PANTOMIME	H.	Tendency
I	9.	DISDAINFULLY	I.	With contempt
P	10.	OBSTINATE	J.	Requested earnestly or solemnly
R	11.	FLUX	K.	Without emotion
S	12.	CESSATION	L.	Came between disputing people; interceded; mediated OR occurred or existed between two things
A	13.	VOLUBILITY	M.	Hypothesis; theory
M	14.	SUPPOSITION	N.	Foolishness
B	15.	CONTAGION	O.	Play or entertainment in which the performers express themselves only by gestures, without speech
T	16.	INDOLENT	P.	Stubborn
K	17.	STOLID	Q.	Deficient in quantity or quality
Q	18.	MEAGRE	R.	Flow
H	19.	INCLINATION	S.	Temporary or complete stopping
J	20.	ADJURED	T.	Lazy

Ethan Frome MULTIPLE CHOICE UNIT TEST 2

I. Matching

____ 1. ZEENA   A. She kissed Ned.

____ 2. MATTIE   B. Builds a house as a gift

____ 3. SILVER   C. Ethan's houseguest

____ 4. FROME   D. Left Ruth a widow

____ 5. HARMON   E. Mrs. Frome

____ 6. NURSE   F. Zeena's relative: Aunt _____

____ 7. DENIS   G. He drove the trunk to the station.

____ 8. EADY   H. Stagecoach driver

____ 9. BETTSBRIDGE   I. Dr. Buck's recommendation for Zeena

____ 10. MOTHER   J. Gave Zeena pickle dish: Aunt _____

____ 11. JOTHAM   K. Zeena's destination

____ 12. SERVANT   L. Wealthy family in Starkfield

____ 13. DANIEL   M. Zeena's first role in the Frome household

____ 14. RUTH   N. Ethan sees himself as a ___.

____ 15. NED   O. Object of Ethan's desire

____ 16. HALE   P. Surname of Ethan

____ 17. PRISONER   Q. Hired hand

____ 18. MARTHA   R. Went insane due to silence

____ 19. NARRATOR   S. Wants to take Mattie on a sleigh ride

____ 20. PHILURA   T. Surname of Mattie

II. Multiple Choice

1. Why is the narrator in Starkfield?
   A. The narrator was sent by his employers on a job related to building a saw-mill.
   B. The narrator was sent by his employers on a job related to breeding horses.
   C. The narrator was sent by his employers on a job related to building a power-house.
   D. The narrator was sent by his employers on a job related to building a railroad.

2. The narrator lodges with Mrs. Ned Hale, what is he hoping to learn from her?
   A. He is hoping Mrs. Hale will tell him all about Zeena and her life.
   B. He is hoping Mrs. Hale will tell him all about Mattie's father.
   C. He is hoping Mrs. Hale will tell him all about Ethan and his life.
   D. He is hoping Mrs. Hale will tell him where her husband hides his money.

3. For what reason does Ethan offer the narrator lodging?
   A. The narrator's inn burns down.
   B. Jotham cannot provide lodging.
   C. Ethan's wife is eager for company.
   D. The snow and cold have made the ride too dangerous.

4. Why does Ethan sneak up and look in the church window?
   A. He has come to bring Zeena home, and he is watching her dance with Denis Eady.
   B. He has come to town for the dance, but he is afraid to go in.
   C. He has come to bring Mattie home, and he is watching her dance with Denis Eady.
   D. He is watching Mattie dance with Jotham.

5. Why is Mattie living with Ethan and Zeena?
   A. Mattie is Zenna's cousin, and she is there to help keep the books at the saw-mill.
   B. Mattie is Zenna's cousin, and she is there to help Zeena.
   C. Mattie is Ethan's cousin, and she is there to help Zeena.
   D. Mattie is Zenna's cousin, and she is there to help take care of Ethan.

6. What happened to Ruth Varnum and Ned Hale while coasting?
   A. Ruth was killed, and Ned was crippled.
   B. Ned was killed, and Ruth was crippled.
   C. Ruth and Ned were killed.
   D. Ruth and Ned were almost killed.

7. Why does Zeena travel to Bettsbridge?
    A. To have an operation
    B. To test Ethan's fidelity
    C. To consult with a doctor
    D. To buy goods for the farm

8. Ethan tells Zeena he can not take her to the train in Corbury Flats because he has to collect money from Mr. Hale for the lumber. Why does he regret this lie?
    A. Zeena is going to Bettsbridge and will buy new clothes.
    B. He will have to give the money to Zeena before she leaves.
    C. Zeena is going to see the doctor and may spend more money than they actually have.
    D. He knows that Zeena will learn the truth when she talks to Mrs. Hale.

9. On what did Ethan and Zeena agree when they were married?
    A. Ethan would care for Zeena's illnesses.
    B. They would put an addition on the house.
    C. They would sell the farm and saw-mill and move to a large town.
    D. They would have two children.

10. About what does Mattie worry while sewing next to Ethan?
    A. Mattie worries that she will not get the sewing done.
    B. Mattie worries that Zeena has something against her.
    C. Mattie worries that Jotham will kiss her.
    D. Mattie worries that Denis Eady will propose.

11. What does Ethan initially think when Zeena remarks that she is very ill?
    A. He hopes it is not true.
    B. He recalls how much he loved Zeena.
    C. He remembers his mother's pain.
    D. He hopes it is true.

12. What realization causes Ethan's sense of helplessness after his conversation with Zeena concerning Mattie?
    A. Zeena is never going to change her mind.
    B. Zeena will live forever.
    C. Ethan will always be trapped in Starkfield.
    D. Mattie is a terrible housekeeper.

13. What does Zeena discover while looking for her stomach powders?
    A. The broken red pickle dish
    B. Fifty dollars
    C. Ethan's train tickets
    D. Love letters

14. Ethan intends to manipulate Mr. Hale into giving Ethan the money he owes for the lumber. What changes Ethan's mind?
    A. Because of Mr. Hale's kindness he realizes he can not take advantage of the Hales.
    B. Ethan decides to steal the money from Denis Eady.
    C. Because of Mrs. Hale's kindness he realizes he can not take advantage of the Hales.
    D. He is too embarrassed to ask the Hales for money.

15. What "illusion" does Ethan have by the pond?
    A. He is going west by train.
    B. This has all been a dream.
    C. He is rich and can afford a divorce.
    D. He is free to marry and is wooing Mattie, the girl he meant to marry.

16. What does Mattie tell Ethan they can do so they will never have to leave each other?
    A. They should kill themselves.
    B. They should go to the train station and run away together.
    C. They should poison Zeena.
    D. They should steal money from Andrew Hale.

17. What are the narrator's observations about the kitchen when he arrives at the Frome household with Ethan?
    A. It is cold and poorly-appointed.
    B. It is the heart of the home.
    C. It is too warm.
    D. It is comforting and welcoming.

18. Whom does Mrs. Hale believe has suffered most from the "accident"?
    A. Ethan
    B. Mattie
    C. Jotham
    D. Zeena

19. What about the "accident" does Mrs. Hale say is a pity?
    A. Mattie became crippled.
    B. Mattie became bitter.
    C. Mattie lived.
    D. Mattie died.

20. To whom does Mrs. Hale compare Ethan, Zeena, and Mattie?
    A. Those who suffered in the Civil War
    B. The ill-fated lovers, Romeo and Juliet
    C. Adam and Eve
    D. The Fromes in the graveyard

III. Essay
1. How are Zeena and Mattie foils for one another?

IV. Vocabulary

___ 1. TACITURNITY   A. Quickly
___ 2. SARDONICALLY   B. Slowly; lacking spirit or liveliness
___ 3. INCREDULOUS   C. Sociable
___ 4. NIMBLY   D. Pretended
___ 5. PRETEXT   E. Natural dislike or aversion
___ 6. CONVIVIAL   F. Complaining
___ 7. PATHOLOGICAL   G. Pass, in reference to time
___ 8. IMPRUDENCE   H. Sacred
___ 9. FEIGNED   I. Mockingly
___ 10. ELAPSE   J. Excuse put forward to conceal a true purpose or object
___ 11. SPECTRAL   K. Guilty uneasiness
___ 12. LANGUIDLY   L. Having few words to say
___ 13. DERISION   M. Free from emotional agitation or nervous tension
___ 14. CONSECRATED   N. Lacking in variety; tediously unvarying
___ 15. ANTIPATHY   O. Act lacking careful consideration or caution
___ 16. COMPUNCTION   P. Relating to diseases or abnormal health
___ 17. UNPERTURBED   Q. Goodwill; kindness
___ 18. BENEVOLENCE   R. Skeptical; unbelieving
___ 19. MONOTONOUS   S. Mocking
___ 20. QUERULOUS   T. Ghostly

Ethan Frome MULTIPLE CHOICE UNIT TEST 2 Answer Key

I. Matching

E	1.	ZEENA	A.	She kissed Ned.
O	2.	MATTIE	B.	Builds a house as a gift
T	3.	SILVER	C.	Ethan's houseguest
P	4.	FROME	D.	Left Ruth a widow
H	5.	HARMON	E.	Mrs. Frome
M	6.	NURSE	F.	Zeena's relative: Aunt _____
S	7.	DENIS	G.	He drove the trunk to the station.
L	8.	EADY	H.	Stagecoach driver
K	9.	BETTSBRIDGE	I.	Dr. Buck's recommendation for Zeena
R	10.	MOTHER	J.	Gave Zeena pickle dish: Aunt _____
Q	11.	JOTHAM	K.	Zeena's destination
I	12.	SERVANT	L.	Wealthy family in Starkfield
G	13.	DANIEL	M.	Zeena's first role in the Frome household
A	14.	RUTH	N.	Ethan sees himself as a ___.
D	15.	NED	O.	Object of Ethan's desire
B	16.	HALE	P.	Surname of Ethan
N	17.	PRISONER	Q.	Hired hand
F	18.	MARTHA	R.	Went insane due to silence
C	19.	NARRATOR	S.	Wants to take Mattie on a sleigh ride
J	20.	PHILURA	T.	Surname of Mattie

II. Multiple Choice

C 1. Why is the narrator in Starkfield?
- A. The narrator was sent by his employers on a job related to building a saw-mill.
- B. The narrator was sent by his employers on a job related to breeding horses.
- C. The narrator was sent by his employers on a job related to building a power-house.
- D. The narrator was sent by his employers on a job related to building a railroad.

C 2. The narrator lodges with Mrs. Ned Hale, what is he hoping to learn from her?
- A. He is hoping Mrs. Hale will tell him all about Zeena and her life.
- B. He is hoping Mrs. Hale will tell him all about Mattie's father.
- C. He is hoping Mrs. Hale will tell him all about Ethan and his life.
- D. He is hoping Mrs. Hale will tell him where her husband hides his money.

D 3. For what reason does Ethan offer the narrator lodging?
- A. The narrator's inn burns down.
- B. Jotham cannot provide lodging.
- C. Ethan's wife is eager for company.
- D. The snow and cold have made the ride too dangerous.

C 4. Why does Ethan sneak up and look in the church window?
- A. He has come to bring Zeena home, and he is watching her dance with Denis Eady.
- B. He has come to town for the dance, but he is afraid to go in.
- C. He has come to bring Mattie home, and he is watching her dance with Denis Eady.
- D. He is watching Mattie dance with Jotham.

B 5. Why is Mattie living with Ethan and Zeena?
- A. Mattie is Zenna's cousin, and she is there to help keep the books at the saw-mill.
- B. Mattie is Zenna's cousin, and she is there to help Zeena.
- C. Mattie is Ethan's cousin, and she is there to help Zeena.
- D. Mattie is Zenna's cousin, and she is there to help take care of Ethan.

D 6. What happened to Ruth Varnum and Ned Hale while coasting?
- A. Ruth was killed, and Ned was crippled.
- B. Ned was killed, and Ruth was crippled.
- C. Ruth and Ned were killed.
- D. Ruth and Ned were almost killed.

C 7. Why does Zeena travel to Bettsbridge?
- A. To have an operation
- B. To test Ethan's fidelity
- C. To consult with a doctor
- D. To buy goods for the farm

C 8. Ethan tells Zeena he can not take her to the train in Corbury Flats because he has to collect money from Mr. Hale for the lumber. Why does he regret this lie?
- A. Zeena is going to Bettsbridge and will buy new clothes.
- B. He will have to give the money to Zeena before she leaves.
- C. Zeena is going to see the doctor and may spend more money than they actually have.
- D. He knows that Zeena will learn the truth when she talks to Mrs. Hale.

C 9. On what did Ethan and Zeena agree when they were married?
- A. Ethan would care for Zeena's illnesses.
- B. They would put an addition on the house.
- C. They would sell the farm and saw-mill and move to a large town.
- D. They would have two children.

B 10. About what does Mattie worry while sewing next to Ethan?
- A. Mattie worries that she will not get the sewing done.
- B. Mattie worries that Zeena has something against her.
- C. Mattie worries that Jotham will kiss her.
- D. Mattie worries that Denis Eady will propose.

D 11. What does Ethan initially think when Zeena remarks that she is very ill?
- A. He hopes it is not true.
- B. He recalls how much he loved Zeena.
- C. He remembers his mother's pain.
- D. He hopes it is true.

A 12. What realization causes Ethan's sense of helplessness after his conversation with Zeena concerning Mattie?
- A. Zeena is never going to change her mind.
- B. Zeena will live forever.
- C. Ethan will always be trapped in Starkfield.
- D. Mattie is a terrible housekeeper.

A 13. What does Zeena discover while looking for her stomach powders?
   A. The broken red pickle dish
   B. Fifty dollars
   C. Ethan's train tickets
   D. Love letters

C 14. Ethan intends to manipulate Mr. Hale into giving Ethan the money he owes for the lumber. What changes Ethan's mind?
   A. Because of Mr. Hale's kindness he realizes he can not take advantage of the Hales.
   B. Ethan decides to steal the money from Denis Eady.
   C. Because of Mrs. Hale's kindness he realizes he can not take advantage of the Hales.
   D. He is too embarrassed to ask the Hales for money.

D 15. What "illusion" does Ethan have by the pond?
   A. He is going west by train.
   B. This has all been a dream.
   C. He is rich and can afford a divorce.
   D. He is free to marry and is wooing Mattie, the girl he meant to marry.

A 16. What does Mattie tell Ethan they can do so they will never have to leave each other?
   A. They should kill themselves.
   B. They should go to the train station and run away together.
   C. They should poison Zeena.
   D. They should steal money from Andrew Hale.

A 17. What are the narrator's observations about the kitchen when he arrives at the Frome household with Ethan?
   A. It is cold and poorly-appointed.
   B. It is the heart of the home.
   C. It is too warm.
   D. It is comforting and welcoming.

A 18. Whom does Mrs. Hale believe has suffered most from the "accident"?
   A. Ethan
   B. Mattie
   C. Jotham
   D. Zeena

C 19. What about the "accident" does Mrs. Hale say is a pity?
- A. Mattie became crippled.
- B. Mattie became bitter.
- C. Mattie lived.
- D. Mattie died.

D 20. To whom does Mrs. Hale compare Ethan, Zeena, and Mattie?
- A. Those who suffered in the Civil War
- B. The ill-fated lovers, Romeo and Juliet
- C. Adam and Eve
- D. The Fromes in the graveyard

IV. Vocabulary

L	1.	TACITURNITY	A.	Quickly
I	2.	SARDONICALLY	B.	Slowly; lacking spirit or liveliness
R	3.	INCREDULOUS	C.	Sociable
A	4.	NIMBLY	D.	Pretended
J	5.	PRETEXT	E.	Natural dislike or aversion
C	6.	CONVIVIAL	F.	Complaining
P	7.	PATHOLOGICAL	G.	Pass, in reference to time
O	8.	IMPRUDENCE	H.	Sacred
D	9.	FEIGNED	I.	Mockingly
G	10.	ELAPSE	J.	Excuse put forward to conceal a true purpose or object
T	11.	SPECTRAL	K.	Guilty uneasiness
B	12.	LANGUIDLY	L.	Having few words to say
S	13.	DERISION	M.	Free from emotional agitation or nervous tension
H	14.	CONSECRATED	N.	Lacking in variety; tediously unvarying
E	15.	ANTIPATHY	O.	Act lacking careful consideration or caution
K	16.	COMPUNCTION	P.	Relating to diseases or abnormal health
M	17.	UNPERTURBED	Q.	Goodwill; kindness
Q	18.	BENEVOLENCE	R.	Skeptical; unbelieving
N	19.	MONOTONOUS	S.	Mocking
F	20.	QUERULOUS	T.	Ghostly

UNIT RESOURCE MATERIALS

BULLETIN BOARD IDEAS *Ethan Frome*

1. Save one corner of the board for the best of students' *Ethan Frome* writing assignments.
2. Take one of the word search puzzles from the extra activities packet and with a marker copy it over in a large size on a bulletin board. Write the clue words to find to one side. Invite students prior to and after class to find the words and circle them on the bulletin board.
3. Write several of the most significant quotations from the book onto the board on brightly-colored paper.
4. Make a bulletin board listing the vocabulary words for this unit. As you complete sections of the novel and discuss the vocabulary for each section, write the definitions on the bulletin board. If your board is one that students face frequently, it will help them learn the words.
5. Title the board, "Going for Our Goals." Make a board with quotes about how to set and achieve goals. Make an area for students to put index cards with their goals on them.
6. Collect appropriate pictures from magazines to "cast" the characters of the story. Add quotes of descriptions of the characters. Additionally, the class could make movie posters, including snippets of reviews, for example, "... a truly great book! ... Two thumbs up! ..." and so on.
7. Edith Wharton received a Pulitzer Prize for her work *The Age of Innocence*. Make a bulletin board related to the award, giving information about it, portraits of winners and summaries of winning works. Relatedly, you can make a bulletin board highlighting major "firsts" accomplished by women, as Wharton was the first woman to win a Pulitzer Prize.
8. To underscore the role of winter in the story, have students find quotes about the starkness and bleakness of winter (from both *Ethan Frome* and other works) and write them on cut-out snowflakes. Make a blizzard of quotes on the board and even hang some on string across the room.
9. Make a bulletin board with several vocabulary terms such as irony, metaphor, perspective, climax, denouement, etc., and give examples from fairy tales. Illustrate your examples.
10. Compile information about important issues such as the pressure to conform, family responsibilities, loneliness, and suicide. Post resources for helping others burdened with these problems or how to seek help for oneself.
11. Make a bulletin board about farming in your area. Print information about local producers, make a map of farms surrounding your area, and post statistics about farming in your community. Also include information about how to support local farmers and the benefits of purchasing locally grown food products.

RELATED TOPICS *Ethan Frome*

1. How to set and achieve goals
2. Living with physical disabilities
3. Sucide
4. Medical practices of the late 19th centruy
5. The role of the church in rural communities
6. Family responsibility
7. Transportation in the late 19th century
8. Lumber Mills
9. The role of men in the late 19th century
10. Literary criticism on *Ethan Frome*
11. The role of women in the late 19th century
12. The condition of hypochondria
13. The decline of farming in America
14. Edith Wharton

MORE ACTIVITIES *Ethan Frome*

1. Have students work together to make a time line chronology of the events in the story. Take a large piece of construction paper and on one wall (or however you can physically arrange it in your room) and make the events of the story along it. Students may want to add drawings or cut-out pictures to represent the events (as well as a written statement).

2. Have students design a book cover (front and back and inside flaps) for *Ethan Frome*.

3. Have students design a bulletin board (ready to be put up, not just sketched) for *Ethan Frome*.

4. Have students group the chapters together to show the larger structure of the novel. Have them explain why they chose the divisions they made.

5. Have students choose one chapter of the novel (with sufficient dialogue) to rewrite as a play. In conjunction with this assignment, have students write a composition explaining the difficulties they encountered in changing from one written form to another.

6. Have students write a letter from one character to another, expressing some secret that the character has been keeping.

7. Tell the class that they are producers of a Broadway musical based on *Ethan Frome*. With Ethan's sentimental daydreaming and the ironic twist of the play's end, the text is great raw material for translation into a musical. Assign each small group of 2-3 students a segment of the story. Students will need to write the lyrics to a song that is relevant to their segment. Students should also write a description of the way the song would be staged. For example, are the characters dancing? Are they singing dialogue to one another? (etc.)

8. Have students interview five people (peers, parents, teachers) and ask them about their goals. Do they have a goal? How long have they had it? How do they work on achieving it?

9. Have students write to someone to ask about his or her goals and how the goals are achieved. Students can write to someone from their community (for example, the owner of a local pizzeria) or to an athlete (for example, an Olympic snowboarder) or to anyone they admire.

10. Have students learn to practice caretaking and sympathy for others. Contact a nursing home or hospice and have students make cards of cheer for residents.

11. Rewrite a fairy tale so that it has an ironic rather than "happily-ever-after" ending, just as *Ethan Frome* does.

12. Students can write a monologue based on a passage from the text, and can act it out in costume for the class.

13. Have students write descriptive paragraphs about their experiences sledding. Where did they sled? How old were they? Were they afraid or exhilarated?

14. Ethan desperately wants freedom to follow his own desires in this story. Research the concept of freedom itself. How does the U.S. Constitution define freedom? Research people whose cause it is (or was) to champion freedom, such as Dr. Martin Luther King, Jr. or Nelson Mandela.

15. Research the history of divorce in America. What cultural influences have made divorce more prevalent in American society?

16. Create a genealogical chart to learn about your relatives. Try to include as many generations as you can. Include names and date and place of birth on your chart.

17. Some readers interpret Zeena as an almost witch-like character, because of her seeming lack of motive, her ominous and sinister nature, and the way her cat acts as an agent in her absence. Research the archetype of witches and familiars in New England literature.
18. Learn about spinal cord injuries and how to avoid them. Learn about how survivors of spinal cord injuries adapt their lifestyles through rehabilitation. Learn also about the medical field of physiatry, the special branch of medicine specifically dedicated to the diagnosis and treatment of physical disability.

UNIT WORD LIST *Ethan Frome*

No.	Word	Clue/Definition
1.	ALIMONY	Ethan calculated he could pay Zeena this, in the event of a divorce.
2.	BETTSBRIDGE	Zeena's destination
3.	CAT	Breaks the pickle dish
4.	CHERRY	Color of Mattie's scarf
5.	COASTING	Ethan & Mattie ran into a tree while doing this.
6.	DANIEL	He drove the trunk to the station.
7.	DENIS	Wants to take Mattie on a sleigh ride
8.	DISH	It was broken into pieces.
9.	DIVORCE	Ethan wished for this, to be free from Zeena.
10.	DUTY	Ethan has a strong sense of this for his obligations.
11.	EADY	Wealthy family in Starkfield
12.	ELM	The tree
13.	ENGINEERING	Ethan's academic interest
14.	FAMILY	Ethan's burdensome roots in Starkfield
15.	FARM	Not worth anything because it is mortgaged
16.	FLATS	Location of train depot: Corbury ____
17.	FROME	Surname of Ethan
18.	GLUE	Ethan didn't use it soon enough.
19.	HALE	Builds a house as a gift
20.	HARMON	Stagecoach driver
21.	ILLNESS	Preoccupies Zeena's thoughts
22.	JEALOUS	Ethan feels this when watching Denis dance with Mattie.
23.	JOTHAM	Hired hand
24.	KEY	It is not in its usual place.
25.	KISS	Ethan gives one to Mattie's sewing project.
26.	KITCHEN	It's a pity that they're all shut up there'n that one ____.
27.	LETTER	Mattie found an undelivered one from Ethan to Zeena.
28.	LIES	Ethan ____ about the lumber money.
29.	LIMP	Physical trait of Ethan
30.	LOCKET	Ethan recovered this at the picnic.
31.	LUMBER	Mill product
32.	MARE	Slipped on ice
33.	MARRY	Ethan fears Mattie and Denis will do this.
34.	MARTHA	Zeena's relative: Aunt ____
35.	MATTIE	Object of Ethan's desire
36.	MEDICINE	Contents of packages Ethan picks up at the post office
37.	MIRACLE	Zeena's ability to be a caretaker is this.
38.	MORTGAGE	Why Ethan can't get money out of the farm

No.	Word	Clue/Definition
39.	MOTHER	Went insane due to silence
40.	NARRATOR	Ethan's houseguest
41.	NED	Left Ruth a widow
42.	NURSE	Zeena's first role in the Frome household
43.	PHILURA	Gave Zeena pickle dish: Aunt ____
44.	PIANO	Mattie sold it for $50.
45.	PICKLES	The broken dish was for these.
46.	POWER	Where narrator works: _____ house
47.	PRISONER	Ethan sees himself as a ___.
48.	RED	Color of the pickle dish
49.	RIBBON	Adorned Mattie's hair at dinner
50.	ROCKING	Zeena's usual resting place: ____ chair
51.	RUTH	She kissed Ned.
52.	SAW	Frome family business: ____ mill
53.	SERVANT	Dr. Buck's recommendation for Zeena
54.	SHADOW	Where Ethan and Mattie declare their love: ____ Pond
55.	SHAVING	Zeena says this causes Ethan to be late.
56.	SILVER	Surname of Mattie
57.	SLED	Vehicle for suicide
58.	STARKFIELD	Town where Ethan lives
59.	STORM	Forces the narrator to seek lodging
60.	STUDY	Private space for Ethan
61.	SUICIDE	Mattie's plan to always be with Ethan.
62.	SWERVE	Zeena's face caused Ethan to make the sled do this.
63.	SYMPATHY	Ethan believes this is what Zeena wants.
64.	TOMBSTONE	Reminder that Ethan will never escape Starkfield
65.	TRUNK	Mattie's belongings were all in one.
66.	ZEENA	Mrs. Frome

WORD SEARCH Ethan Frome

```
L Q X P F A R M D G Z D I S H A H A P L
I U N A R R A T O R E G P T N X R L G K
E V M E M I C Q O Q N W U E H U M I D X
S K W B L D S W J M O R E R L F A M A T
L O C K E T C O L Q B Z X I D A T O N B
P N W L C R T D N H I S H B C M T N I Z
S A S S O H S A J E A P T B F I I Y E D
T I F L A T S H N Y R G H O W L E C L T
U P L M S S M S R U N P A N N Y F X W D
D L S D T F N R Q I R I L L N E S S L E
Y L A E I D A E V G C S E P P K T C G P
L Q W N N M U A D Y R R E H C N P D M B
L I S I G Y H T A P M Y S G K U I A J N
J E M S N S X G Y O Q B N V B R R Y E N
S D T P L S C W T C C I N G B T X C A N
P I L T R W J H F B K C R S H K R B L Z
P C N W E E T R C R A T A F O I Y O K
S I L V E R S T O R M T N A V R E S U P
T U K H X V E R M D E H P I C K L E S H
H S G L U E Q D E B E A D Y M A R E Q N
```

ALIMONY	FROME	MARTHA	SAW
BETTSBRIDGE	GLUE	MATTIE	SERVANT
CAT	HALE	MOTHER	SHADOW
CHERRY	ILLNESS	NARRATOR	SHAVING
COASTING	JEALOUS	NED	SILVER
DANIEL	JOTHAM	NURSE	SLED
DENIS	KEY	PHILURA	STORM
DISH	KISS	PIANO	STUDY
DIVORCE	LETTER	PICKLES	SUICIDE
DUTY	LIES	POWER	SWERVE
EADY	LIMP	PRISONER	SYMPATHY
ELM	LOCKET	RED	TOMBSTONE
FAMILY	LUMBER	RIBBON	TRUNK
FARM	MARE	ROCKING	ZEENA
FLATS	MARRY	RUTH	

WORD SEARCH ANSWER KEY Ethan Frome

ALIMONY	FROME	MARTHA	SAW
BETTSBRIDGE	GLUE	MATTIE	SERVANT
CAT	HALE	MOTHER	SHADOW
CHERRY	ILLNESS	NARRATOR	SHAVING
COASTING	JEALOUS	NED	SILVER
DANIEL	JOTHAM	NURSE	SLED
DENIS	KEY	PHILURA	STORM
DISH	KISS	PIANO	STUDY
DIVORCE	LETTER	PICKLES	SUICIDE
DUTY	LIES	POWER	SWERVE
EADY	LIMP	PRISONER	SYMPATHY
ELM	LOCKET	RED	TOMBSTONE
FAMILY	LUMBER	RIBBON	TRUNK
FARM	MARE	ROCKING	ZEENA
FLATS	MARRY	RUTH	

CROSSWORD Ethan Frome

Across
1. Ethan's academic interest
7. Mill product
8. Ethan fears Mattie and Denis will do this.
9. Ethan ___ about the lumber money.
11. Ethan gives one to Mattie's sewing project.
12. Reminder that Ethan will never escape Starkfield
14. He drove the trunk to the station.
17. Wants to take Mattie on a sleigh ride
19. Color of the pickle dish
20. Vehicle for suicide
22. Stagecoach driver
24. Mattie's belongings were all in one.
25. Breaks the picke dish
26. Zeena's relative: Aunt ___
27. Mrs. Frome
28. She kissed Ned.

Down
2. Ethan didn't use it soon enough.
3. Left Ruth a widow
4. The tree
5. Zeena's first role in the Frome household
6. Ethan feels this when watching Denis & Mattie dance.
9. Ethan recovered it at the picnic.
10. Forces the narrator to seek lodging
11. It is not in its usual place.
13. Contents of packages Ethan picks up at the post office
15. Ethan's houseguest
16. Wealthy family in Starkfield
17. It was broken to pieces.
18. Preoccupies Zeena's thoughts
21. Ethan has a strong sense of this for his obligations.
22. Builds a house as a gift
23. Zeena's usual resting place: ___ chair
26. Slipped on ice

CROSSWORD ANSWER KEY Ethan Frome

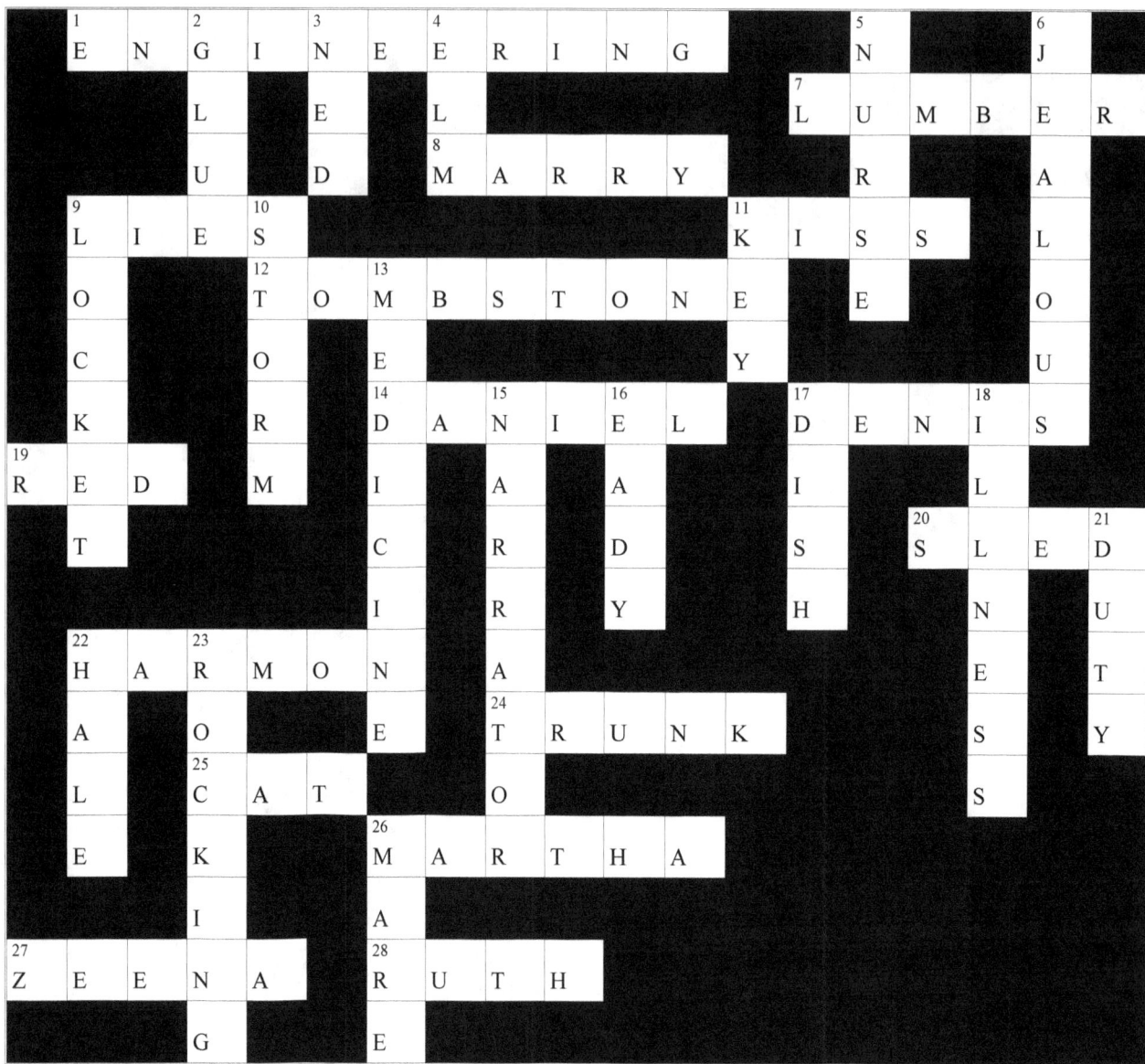

Across
1. Ethan's academic interest
7. Mill product
8. Ethan fears Mattie and Denis will do this.
9. Ethan ___ about the lumber money.
11. Ethan gives one to Mattie's sewing project.
12. Reminder that Ethan will never escape Starkfield
14. He drove the trunk to the station.
17. Wants to take Mattie on a sleigh ride
19. Color of the pickle dish
20. Vehicle for suicide
22. Stagecoach driver
24. Mattie's belongings were all in one.
25. Breaks the pickle dish
26. Zeena's relative: Aunt ___
27. Mrs. Frome
28. She kissed Ned.

Down
2. Ethan didn't use it soon enough.
3. Left Ruth a widow
4. The tree
5. Zeena's first role in the Frome household
6. Ethan feels this when watching Denis & Mattie dance.
9. Ethan recovered it at the picnic.
10. Forces the narrator to seek lodging
11. It is not in its usual place.
13. Contents of packages Ethan picks up at the post office
15. Ethan's houseguest
16. Wealthy family in Starkfield
17. It was broken to pieces.
18. Preoccupies Zeena's thoughts
21. Ethan has a strong sense of this for his obligations.
22. Builds a house as a gift
23. Zeena's usual resting place: ___ chair
26. Slipped on ice

UNIT MATCHING 1 *Ethan Frome*

____ 1. MARTHA   A. Ethan has a strong sense of this for his obligations.

____ 2. MOTHER   B. Went insane due to silence

____ 3. DUTY   C. Mrs. Frome

____ 4. PIANO   D. Physical trait of Ethan

____ 5. SHAVING   E. Ethan gives one to Mattie's sewing project.

____ 6. EADY   F. Why Ethan can't get money out of the farm

____ 7. CHERRY   G. Contents of packages Ethan picks up at the post office

____ 8. MEDICINE   H. Zeena says this causes Ethan to be late.

____ 9. FROME   I. Mattie sold it for $50.

____ 10. DISH   J. It was broken into pieces.

____ 11. SERVANT   K. Zeena's relative: Aunt _____

____ 12. MORTGAGE   L. Surname of Ethan

____ 13. KISS   M. Zeena's ability to be a caretaker is this.

____ 14. SAW   N. Builds a house as a gift

____ 15. LIMP   O. Dr. Buck's recommendation for Zeena

____ 16. TRUNK   P. Color of Mattie's scarf

____ 17. MIRACLE   Q. Wealthy family in Starkfield

____ 18. HALE   R. He drove the trunk to the station.

____ 19. DANIEL   S. Frome family business: ____ mill

____ 20. ZEENA   T. Mattie's belongings were all in one.

UNIT MATCHING 1 ANSWER KEY *Ethan Frome*

K	1.	MARTHA	A.	Ethan has a strong sense of this for his obligations.
B	2.	MOTHER	B.	Went insane due to silence
A	3.	DUTY	C.	Mrs. Frome
I	4.	PIANO	D.	Physical trait of Ethan
H	5.	SHAVING	E.	Ethan gives one to Mattie's sewing project.
Q	6.	EADY	F.	Why Ethan can't get money out of the farm
P	7.	CHERRY	G.	Contents of packages Ethan picks up at the post office
G	8.	MEDICINE	H.	Zeena says this causes Ethan to be late.
L	9.	FROME	I.	Mattie sold it for $50.
J	10.	DISH	J.	It was broken into pieces.
O	11.	SERVANT	K.	Zeena's relative: Aunt _____
F	12.	MORTGAGE	L.	Surname of Ethan
E	13.	KISS	M.	Zeena's ability to be a caretaker is this.
S	14.	SAW	N.	Builds a house as a gift
D	15.	LIMP	O.	Dr. Buck's recommendation for Zeena
T	16.	TRUNK	P.	Color of Mattie's scarf
M	17.	MIRACLE	Q.	Wealthy family in Starkfield
N	18.	HALE	R.	He drove the trunk to the station.
R	19.	DANIEL	S.	Frome family business: _____ mill
C	20.	ZEENA	T.	Mattie's belongings were all in one.

UNIT MATCHING 2 *Ethan Frome*

____ 1. LUMBER   A. Ethan calculated he could pay Zeena this, in the event of a divorce.
____ 2. MARE   B. She kissed Ned.
____ 3. KITCHEN   C. Hired hand
____ 4. BETTSBRIDGE   D. Zeena's first role in the Frome household
____ 5. TOMBSTONE   E. Stagecoach driver
____ 6. COASTING   F. Adorned Mattie's hair at dinner
____ 7. NURSE   G. Where narrator works: _____ house
____ 8. HARMON   H. Vehicle for suicide
____ 9. CAT   I. Slipped on ice
____ 10. JOTHAM   J. Preoccupies Zeena's thoughts
____ 11. ILLNESS   K. It is not in its usual place.
____ 12. ALIMONY   L. Mattie found an undelivered one from Ethan to Zeena.
____ 13. SYMPATHY   M. Mill product
____ 14. RIBBON   N. Ethan & Mattie ran into a tree while doing this.
____ 15. KEY   O. Breaks the pickle dish
____ 16. POWER   P. Zeena's destination
____ 17. LETTER   Q. Ethan believes this is what Zeena wants.
____ 18. SLED   R. Object of Ethan's desire
____ 19. RUTH   S. It's a pity that they're all shut up there'n that one ___.
____ 20. MATTIE   T. Reminder that Ethan will never escape Starkfield

UNIT MATCHING 2 ANSWER KEY *Ethan Frome*

M	1.	LUMBER	A.	Ethan calculated he could pay Zeena this, in the event of a divorce.
I	2.	MARE	B.	She kissed Ned.
S	3.	KITCHEN	C.	Hired hand
P	4.	BETTSBRIDGE	D.	Zeena's first role in the Frome household
T	5.	TOMBSTONE	E.	Stagecoach driver
N	6.	COASTING	F.	Adorned Mattie's hair at dinner
D	7.	NURSE	G.	Where narrator works: _____ house
E	8.	HARMON	H.	Vehicle for suicide
O	9.	CAT	I.	Slipped on ice
C	10.	JOTHAM	J.	Preoccupies Zeena's thoughts
J	11.	ILLNESS	K.	It is not in its usual place.
A	12.	ALIMONY	L.	Mattie found an undelivered one from Ethan to Zeena.
Q	13.	SYMPATHY	M.	Mill product
F	14.	RIBBON	N.	Ethan & Mattie ran into a tree while doing this.
K	15.	KEY	O.	Breaks the pickle dish
G	16.	POWER	P.	Zeena's destination
L	17.	LETTER	Q.	Ethan believes this is what Zeena wants.
H	18.	SLED	R.	Object of Ethan's desire
B	19.	RUTH	S.	It's a pity that they're all shut up there'n that one ___.
R	20.	MATTIE	T.	Reminder that Ethan will never escape Starkfield

UNIT JUGGLE 1 *Ethan Frome*

_____ = 1. RSOMT
Forces the narrator to seek lodging

_____ = 2. LFADKSTERI
Town where Ethan lives

_____ = 3. SYUDT
Private space for Ethan

_____ = 4. DSIEN
Wants to take Mattie on a sleigh ride

_____ = 5. KTOECL
Ethan recovered this at the picnic.

_____ = 6. LSIE
Ethan ___ about the lumber money.

_____ = 7. MYILAF
Ethan's burdensome roots in Starkfield

_____ = 8. YRAMR
Ethan fears Mattie and Denis will do this.

_____ = 9. PLESCKI
The broken dish was for these.

_____ = 10. LUGE
Ethan didn't use it soon enough.

_____ = 11. VICDERO
Ethan wished for this, to be free from Zeena.

_____ = 12. NDE
Left Ruth a widow

_____ = 13. SVEWRE
Zeena's face caused Ethan to make the sled do this.

_____ = 14. MAFR
Not worth anything because it is mortgaged

_____ = 15. SIVELR
Surname of Mattie

UNIT JUGGLE 1 ANSWER KEY *Ethan Frome*

STORM	= 1.	RSOMT Forces the narrator to seek lodging
STARKFIELD	= 2.	LFADKSTERI Town where Ethan lives
STUDY	= 3.	SYUDT Private space for Ethan
DENIS	= 4.	DSIEN Wants to take Mattie on a sleigh ride
LOCKET	= 5.	KTOECL Ethan recovered this at the picnic.
LIES	= 6.	LSIE Ethan ___ about the lumber money.
FAMILY	= 7.	MYILAF Ethan's burdensome roots in Starkfield
MARRY	= 8.	YRAMR Ethan fears Mattie and Denis will do this.
PICKLES	= 9.	PLESCKI The broken dish was for these.
GLUE	= 10.	LUGE Ethan didn't use it soon enough.
DIVORCE	= 11.	VICDERO Ethan wished for this, to be free from Zeena.
NED	= 12.	NDE Left Ruth a widow
SWERVE	= 13.	SVEWRE Zeena's face caused Ethan to make the sled do this.
FARM	= 14.	MAFR Not worth anything because it is mortgaged
SILVER	= 15.	SIVELR Surname of Mattie

UNIT JUGGLE 2 *Ethan Frome*

_____ = 1. RUHILAP
Gave Zeena pickle dish: Aunt ____

_____ = 2. DETIBBRGTSE
Zeena's destination

_____ = 3. JTHMOA
Hired hand

_____ = 4. ARLCEMI
Zeena's ability to be a caretaker is this.

_____ = 5. EOAUJLS
Ethan feels this when watching Denis dance with Mattie.

_____ = 6. GRNCIOK
Zeena's usual resting place: ____ chair

_____ = 7. NISPORRE
Ethan sees himself as a ___.

_____ = 8. IDCUIES
Mattie's plan to always be with Ethan.

_____ = 9. DRE
Color of the pickle dish

_____ = 10. NRGIIEEGNNE
Ethan's academic interest

_____ = 11. LTSFA
Location of train depot: Corbury ____

_____ = 12. AOHWSD
Where Ethan and Mattie declare their love: ____ Pond

_____ = 13. EML
The tree

_____ = 14. AARNORRT
Ethan's houseguest

_____ = 15. TLDASEIKFR
Town where Ethan lives

171

UNIT JUGGLE 2 ANSWER KEY *Ethan Frome*

PHILURA	= 1.	RUHILAP Gave Zeena pickle dish: Aunt ____
BETTSBRIDGE	= 2.	DETIBBRGTSE Zeena's destination
JOTHAM	= 3.	JTHMOA Hired hand
MIRACLE	= 4.	ARLCEMI Zeena's ability to be a caretaker is this.
JEALOUS	= 5.	EOAUJLS Ethan feels this when watching Denis dance with Mattie.
ROCKING	= 6.	GRNCIOK Zeena's usual resting place: ____ chair
PRISONER	= 7.	NISPORRE Ethan sees himself as a ___.
SUICIDE	= 8.	IDCUIES Mattie's plan to always be with Ethan.
RED	= 9.	DRE Color of the pickle dish
ENGINEERING	= 10.	NRGIIEEGNNE Ethan's academic interest
FLATS	= 11.	LTSFA Location of train depot: Corbury ____
SHADOW	= 12.	AOHWSD Where Ethan and Mattie declare their love: ____ Pond
ELM	= 13.	EML The tree
NARRATOR	= 14.	AARNORRT Ethan's houseguest
STARKFIELD	= 15.	TLDASEIKFR Town where Ethan lives

VOCABULARY RESOURCE MATERIALS

Ethan Frome Vocabulary

No.	Word	Clue/Definition
1.	ADJURED	Requested earnestly or solemnly
2.	ALLUSION	Casual reference
3.	ANTIPATHY	Natural dislike or aversion
4.	AUDACITY	Arrogant boldness or daring
5.	AUSTERE	Severely simple; without ornament; lacking softness
6.	BENEVOLENCE	Goodwill; kindness
7.	CESSATION	Temporary or complete stopping
8.	COMPENSATION	Something given or received as an equivalent for services, debt, loss, injury, suffering, lack, etc.
9.	COMPUNCTION	Guilty uneasiness
10.	CONCLUSIVE	Serving to settle or decide a question; decisive; convincing
11.	CONSECRATED	Sacred
12.	CONSPIRE	Jointly make secret plans to commit an unlawful or harmful act
13.	CONTAGION	Transmission or spread of an idea, emotion, or disease from person to person
14.	CONVIVIAL	Sociable
15.	DEMURRED	Raised doubts or objections
16.	DERISION	Mocking
17.	DISDAINFULLY	With contempt
18.	DIVINED	Guessed using intuition or insight
19.	EFFRONTERY	Boldness
20.	ELAPSE	Pass, in reference to time
21.	ELUDED	Avoided; escaped
22.	EXANIMATE	Lifeless
23.	EXPEDITIONS	Journeys undertaken with a purpose
24.	FATUITY	Foolishness
25.	FEIGNED	Pretended
26.	FELICITOUS	Well-suited for the occasion, as an action, manner, or expression; appropriate
27.	FLUX	Flow
28.	FOIST	Force or impose upon fraudulently or unjustifiably
29.	IMPRUDENCE	Act lacking careful consideration or caution
30.	INCLINATION	Tendency
31.	INCREDULOUS	Skeptical; unbelieving
32.	INDIGNATION	Anger due to injustice
33.	INDOLENT	Lazy
34.	INDUCED	Moved by persuasion or influence
35.	INJUNCTION	Command
36.	INTERCOURSE	Communications

No.	Word	Clue/Definition
37.	INTERVENED	Came between disputing people; interceded; mediated OR occurred or existed between two things
38.	LANGUIDLY	Slowly; lacking spirit or liveliness
39.	LOTH	Reluctant; unwilling
40.	MEAGRE	Deficient in quantity or quality
41.	MIEN	Demeanor; manner
42.	MONOTONOUS	Lacking in variety; tediously unvarying
43.	NIMBLY	Quickly
44.	OBSTINATE	Stubborn
45.	OMISSIONS	Things left out or undone
46.	OPULENCE	Wealth; riches
47.	PANTOMIME	Play or entertainment in which the performers express themselves only by gestures, without speech
48.	PATHOLOGICAL	Relating to diseases or abnormal health
49.	PERFUNCTORY	Hasty and superficial
50.	POIGNANT	Keenly distressing to the emotions
51.	PRECEDENT	Act, decision, or case that serves as a guide or justification for subsequent situations
52.	PRETEXT	Excuse put forward to conceal a true purpose or object
53.	QUERULOUS	Complaining
54.	REVELRY	Celebration
55.	SALLOW	Sickly, yellowish color
56.	SARDONICALLY	Mockingly
57.	SCINTILLATING	Dazzling
58.	SPECTRAL	Ghostly
59.	SQUALID	Foul and repulsive, as from lack of care or cleanliness
60.	STOLID	Without emotion
61.	SUFFUSED	Spread through
62.	SUPERSEDED	Replaced
63.	SUPPOSITION	Hypothesis; theory
64.	TACITURNITY	Having few words to say
65.	TREMULOUS	Characterized by trembling, as from fear, nervousness, or weakness
66.	UNPERTURBED	Free from emotional agitation or nervous tension
67.	VOLUBILITY	Talkativeness

VOCABULARY WORD SEARCH Ethan Frome

```
D E R I S I O N S U P P O S I T I O N S
T V B C J W L A I V I V N O C A A Y N M
S B P O P A Q H G K A Z W B S C N X H P
L J Z N O Q U E R U L O U S U I T T L T
C D N T I W L D K R L P N T F T I A J
M G Y A G F L S A K U H I I F U P N C L
D O R G N K K Q L C S Y M N U R A D I V
A X N I A V F U K W I M B A S N T I G P
R D G O N A O A O N O T L T E I H G O L
J I J N T N E L O D N I Y E D T Y N L H
D L A U Q O L I U P E L B X O Y K A O V
Y O I U R A N D G B D X P L S R R T H K
P T F Q S E C O F I I U A N M T M I T F
Y S S D L T D O U O P L Q N C I N O A J
F Z B U Z Y E G N S I F I E I D E N P P
D F D P T J N R L S J S P T U M H N C G
Z E C F B A T D E Y P S T C Y Y A G G N
D S U O L U D E R C N I E R N M S T V Z
M E A G R E L A P S E D R Y R L E V E R
I N C L I N A T I O N P D E M U R R E D
```

ADJURED	FLUX	PATHOLOGICAL
ALLUSION	FOIST	POIGNANT
ANTIPATHY	INCLINATION	QUERULOUS
AUDACITY	INCREDULOUS	REVELRY
AUSTERE	INDIGNATION	SALLOW
CONSPIRE	INDOLENT	SPECTRAL
CONTAGION	INDUCED	SQUALID
CONVIVIAL	LANGUIDLY	STOLID
DEMURRED	LOTH	SUFFUSED
DERISION	MEAGRE	SUPPOSITION
ELAPSE	MIEN	TACITURNITY
ELUDED	MONOTONOUS	VOLUBILITY
EXANIMATE	NIMBLY	
FATUITY	OBSTINATE	

VOCABULARY WORD SEARCH ANSWER KEY Ethan Frome

```
D E R I S I O N S U P P O S I T I O N
    C         L A I V I V N O C A   A
    O   P   A             A   B S C   N
    N   O Q U E R U L O U S   U I T   L
    T   I     D       L   N   F T I   A
M   A   G     S   A   U   I   F U P   C
  O   G N     Q       C   M   U R A   I
A   N   I A V F U   W I   B   A S T I G
  D   O N A O A O   T L   T   E I H G O
    I J N T N E L O D N I Y   D T Y N L
      L A U O L I U     E L     O Y   A O
        O I U R A N D   B D X   L     R T H
          T   S E C O F I I U A   M   I   T
        Y S   L T D O U O   L   N C   N O A
              U   E G N S I F   I E   D N P
            D     N R   S     S P T U M N
              E       A     R E P S T C Y A T
          D S U O L U D E R C N I E         T
          M E A G R E L A P S E D R Y R L E V E R
          I N C L I N A T I O N     D E M U R R E D
```

ADJURED
ALLUSION
ANTIPATHY
AUDACITY
AUSTERE
CONSPIRE
CONTAGION
CONVIVIAL
DEMURRED
DERISION
ELAPSE
ELUDED
EXANIMATE
FATUITY

FLUX
FOIST
INCLINATION
INCREDULOUS
INDIGNATION
INDOLENT
INDUCED
LANGUIDLY
LOTH
MEAGRE
MIEN
MONOTONOUS
NIMBLY
OBSTINATE

PATHOLOGICAL
POIGNANT
QUERULOUS
REVELRY
SALLOW
SPECTRAL
SQUALID
STOLID
SUFFUSED
SUPPOSITION
TACITURNITY
VOLUBILITY

VOCABULARY CROSSWORD Ethan Frome

Across
1. Temporary or complete stopping
8. Lazy
11. Reluctant; unwilling
12. Demeanor; manner
13. Foolishness
14. Force or impose upon fraudulently or unjustifiably
16. Requested earnestly or solemnly
19. Excuse put forward to conceal a true purpose or object
21. Flow
22. Arrogant boldness or daring
23. Came between disputing people; interceded; mediated OR occurred or existed between two things
24. Moved by persuasion or influence

Down
1. Sacred
2. Sickly, yellowish color
3. Natural dislike or aversion
4. Act lacking careful consideration or caution
5. Quickly
6. Pass, in reference to time
7. Tendency
9. Raised doubts or objections
10. Without emotion
12. Deficient in quantity or quality
15. Ghostly
16. Casual reference
17. Celebration
18. Mocking
20. Avoided; escaped

VOCABULARY CROSSWORD ANSWER KEY Ethan Frome

Across
1. Temporary or complete stopping
8. Lazy
11. Reluctant; unwilling
12. Demeanor; manner
13. Foolishness
14. Force or impose upon fraudulently or unjustifiably
16. Requested earnestly or solemnly
19. Excuse put forward to conceal a true purpose or object
21. Flow
22. Arrogant boldness or daring
23. Came between disputing people; interceded; mediated OR occurred or existed between two things
24. Moved by persuasion or influence

Down
1. Sacred
2. Sickly, yellowish color
3. Natural dislike or aversion
4. Act lacking careful consideration or caution
5. Quickly
6. Pass, in reference to time
7. Tendency
9. Raised doubts or objections
10. Without emotion
12. Deficient in quantity or quality
15. Ghostly
16. Casual reference
17. Celebration
18. Mocking
20. Avoided; escaped

VOCAB MATCHING 1 *Ethan Frome*

___ 1. UNPERTURBED   A. Arrogant boldness or daring

___ 2. FELICITOUS   B. Free from emotional agitation or nervous tension

___ 3. EXPEDITIONS   C. Transmission or spread of an idea, emotion, or disease from person to person

___ 4. ELAPSE   D. Well-suited for the occasion, as an action, manner, or expression; appropriate

___ 5. DISDAINFULLY   E. Pass, in reference to time

___ 6. CONTAGION   F. Anger due to injustice

___ 7. CONCLUSIVE   G. Keenly distressing to the emotions

___ 8. CESSATION   H. Temporary or complete stopping

___ 9. AUDACITY   I. Mockingly

___ 10. IMPRUDENCE   J. Foul and repulsive, as from lack of care or cleanliness

___ 11. INDIGNATION   K. Command

___ 12. SQUALID   L. Demeanor; manner

___ 13. SARDONICALLY   M. Play or entertainment in which the performers express themselves only by gestures, without speech

___ 14. QUERULOUS   N. Serving to settle or decide a question; decisive; convincing

___ 15. POIGNANT   O. With contempt

___ 16. PANTOMIME   P. Slowly; lacking spirit or liveliness

___ 17. MIEN   Q. Requested earnestly or solemnly

___ 18. LANGUIDLY   R. Journeys undertaken with a purpose

___ 19. INJUNCTION   S. Complaining

___ 20. ADJURED   T. Act lacking careful consideration or caution

VOCAB MATCHING 1 ANSWER KEY *Ethan Frome*

B	1.	UNPERTURBED	A.	Arrogant boldness or daring
D	2.	FELICITOUS	B.	Free from emotional agitation or nervous tension
R	3.	EXPEDITIONS	C.	Transmission or spread of an idea, emotion, or disease from person to person
E	4.	ELAPSE	D.	Well-suited for the occasion, as an action, manner, or expression; appropriate
O	5.	DISDAINFULLY	E.	Pass, in reference to time
C	6.	CONTAGION	F.	Anger due to injustice
N	7.	CONCLUSIVE	G.	Keenly distressing to the emotions
H	8.	CESSATION	H.	Temporary or complete stopping
A	9.	AUDACITY	I.	Mockingly
T	10.	IMPRUDENCE	J.	Foul and repulsive, as from lack of care or cleanliness
F	11.	INDIGNATION	K.	Command
J	12.	SQUALID	L.	Demeanor; manner
I	13.	SARDONICALLY	M.	Play or entertainment in which the performers express themselves only by gestures, without speech
S	14.	QUERULOUS	N.	Serving to settle or decide a question; decisive; convincing
G	15.	POIGNANT	O.	With contempt
M	16.	PANTOMIME	P.	Slowly; lacking spirit or liveliness
L	17.	MIEN	Q.	Requested earnestly or solemnly
P	18.	LANGUIDLY	R.	Journeys undertaken with a purpose
K	19.	INJUNCTION	S.	Complaining
Q	20.	ADJURED	T.	Act lacking careful consideration or caution

VOCAB MATCHING 2 *Ethan Frome*

____ 1. VOLUBILITY   A. Talkativeness

____ 2. FLUX   B. Spread through

____ 3. FATUITY   C. Relating to diseases or abnormal health

____ 4. ELUDED   D. Severely simple; without ornament; lacking softness

____ 5. DIVINED   E. Communications

____ 6. CONVIVIAL   F. Lazy

____ 7. CONSECRATED   G. Flow

____ 8. COMPENSATION   H. Sacred

____ 9. AUSTERE   I. Guessed using intuition or insight

____ 10. INCLINATION   J. Sociable

____ 11. INDOLENT   K. Having few words to say

____ 12. TACITURNITY   L. Avoided; escaped

____ 13. SUFFUSED   M. Lacking in variety; tediously unvarying

____ 14. PRECEDENT   N. Reluctant; unwilling

____ 15. PATHOLOGICAL   O. Foolishness

____ 16. OMISSIONS   P. Things left out or undone

____ 17. MONOTONOUS   Q. Act, decision, or case that serves as a guide or justification for subsequent situations

____ 18. LOTH   R. Casual reference

____ 19. INTERCOURSE   S. Something given or received as an equivalent for services, debt, loss, injury, suffering, lack, etc.

____ 20. ALLUSION   T. Tendency

VOCAB MATCHING 2 ANSWER KEY *Ethan Frome*

A	1.	VOLUBILITY	A.	Talkativeness
G	2.	FLUX	B.	Spread through
O	3.	FATUITY	C.	Relating to diseases or abnormal health
L	4.	ELUDED	D.	Severely simple; without ornament; lacking softness
I	5.	DIVINED	E.	Communications
J	6.	CONVIVIAL	F.	Lazy
H	7.	CONSECRATED	G.	Flow
S	8.	COMPENSATION	H.	Sacred
D	9.	AUSTERE	I.	Guessed using intuition or insight
T	10.	INCLINATION	J.	Sociable
F	11.	INDOLENT	K.	Having few words to say
K	12.	TACITURNITY	L.	Avoided; escaped
B	13.	SUFFUSED	M.	Lacking in variety; tediously unvarying
Q	14.	PRECEDENT	N.	Reluctant; unwilling
C	15.	PATHOLOGICAL	O.	Foolishness
P	16.	OMISSIONS	P.	Things left out or undone
M	17.	MONOTONOUS	Q.	Act, decision, or case that serves as a guide or justification for subsequent situations
N	18.	LOTH	R.	Casual reference
E	19.	INTERCOURSE	S.	Something given or received as an equivalent for services, debt, loss, injury, suffering, lack, etc.
R	20.	ALLUSION	T.	Tendency

VOCAB JUGGLE 1 *Ethan Frome*

_____ = 1. NMLIYB
Quickly

_____ = 2. EOEENCNELBV
Goodwill; kindness

_____ = 3. CCOUNMIPONT
Guilty uneasiness

_____ = 4. CSNROIPE
Jointly make secret plans to commit an unlawful or harmful act

_____ = 5. RUERDMDE
Raised doubts or objections

_____ = 6. IDSRENIO
Mocking

_____ = 7. YFOTRFENER
Boldness

_____ = 8. ANATXMIEE
Lifeless

_____ = 9. FNGEDEI
Pretended

_____ = 10. SFITO
Force or impose upon fraudulently or unjustifiably

_____ = 11. UNSCREOIUDL
Skeptical; unbelieving

_____ = 12. DDUECIN
Moved by persuasion or influence

_____ = 13. DEETIENVRN
Came between disputing people; interceded; mediated OR occurred or existed between two things

_____ = 14. RGEAME
Deficient in quantity or quality

_____ = 15. YAAPNTITH
Natural dislike or aversion

VOCAB JUGGLE 1 ANSWER KEY *Ethan Frome*

NIMBLY	= 1.	NMLIYB Quickly
BENEVOLENCE	= 2.	EOEENCNELBV Goodwill; kindness
COMPUNCTION	= 3.	CCOUNMIPONT Guilty uneasiness
CONSPIRE	= 4.	CSNROIPE Jointly make secret plans to commit an unlawful or harmful act
DEMURRED	= 5.	RUERDMDE Raised doubts or objections
DERISION	= 6.	IDSRENIO Mocking
EFFRONTERY	= 7.	YFOTRFENER Boldness
EXANIMATE	= 8.	ANATXMIEE Lifeless
FEIGNED	= 9.	FNGEDEI Pretended
FOIST	= 10.	SFITO Force or impose upon fraudulently or unjustifiably
INCREDULOUS	= 11.	UNSCREOIUDL Skeptical; unbelieving
INDUCED	= 12.	DDUECIN Moved by persuasion or influence
INTERVENED	= 13.	DEETIENVRN Came between disputing people; interceded; mediated OR occurred or existed between two things
MEAGRE	= 14.	RGEAME Deficient in quantity or quality
ANTIPATHY	= 15.	YAAPNTITH Natural dislike or aversion

VOCAB JUGGLE 2 *Ethan Frome*

_____ = 1. UTDERUEPBRN
Free from emotional agitation or nervous tension

_____ = 2. DEUDEL
Avoided; escaped

_____ = 3. UITATYF
Foolishness

_____ = 4. ELCUONPE
Wealth; riches

_____ = 5. YUOPCFTRNRE
Hasty and superficial

_____ = 6. RTEPTEX
Excuse put forward to conceal a true purpose or object

_____ = 7. VEELYRR
Celebration

_____ = 8. SOLWLA
Sickly, yellowish color

_____ = 9. IIALIGTTNSCNL
Dazzling

_____ = 10. TRPLSAEC
Ghostly

_____ = 11. ITDLOS
Without emotion

_____ = 12. SEEUDDSERP
Replaced

_____ = 13. OUPSITINSPO
Hypothesis; theory

_____ = 14. UTLSRMOEU
Characterized by trembling, as from fear, nervousness, or weakness

_____ = 15. CRDAOCENSET
Sacred

VOCAB JUGGLE 2 ANSWER KEY *Ethan Frome*

UNPERTURBED	= 1.	UTDERUEPBRN Free from emotional agitation or nervous tension
ELUDED	= 2.	DEUDEL Avoided; escaped
FATUITY	= 3.	UITATYF Foolishness
OPULENCE	= 4.	ELCUONPE Wealth; riches
PERFUNCTORY	= 5.	YUOPCFTRNRE Hasty and superficial
PRETEXT	= 6.	RTEPTEX Excuse put forward to conceal a true purpose or object
REVELRY	= 7.	VEELYRR Celebration
SALLOW	= 8.	SOLWLA Sickly, yellowish color
SCINTILLATING	= 9.	IIALIGTTNSCNL Dazzling
SPECTRAL	= 10.	TRPLSAEC Ghostly
STOLID	= 11.	ITDLOS Without emotion
SUPERSEDED	= 12.	SEEUDDSERP Replaced
SUPPOSITION	= 13.	OUPSITINSPO Hypothesis; theory
TREMULOUS	= 14.	UTLSRMOEU Characterized by trembling, as from fear, nervousness, or weakness
CONSECRATED	= 15.	CRDAOCENSET Sacred

www.ingramcontent.com/pod-product-compliance
Lightning Source LLC
LaVergne TN
LVHW081533060526
838200LV00048B/2069